Looking Back in Lavender Bay

The Lavender Bay Chronicles Book 5

Michele Brouder

This is a work of fiction.

Names, characters, places and incidents are either a product of the author's imagination or are used fictitiously, and any resemblance to actual persons, living or dead, events, or locales is entirely coincidental.

Editing by Jessica Peirce
Book Cover Design by Rebecca Ruger

Looking Back in Lavender Bay © 2025 Michele Brouder

All Rights Reserved. No part of this book may be reproduced or transmitted in any form or by any means, electronic or mechanical, including photocopying, recording, or by any information storage and retrieval system, without permission in writing from the author.

To God be the Glory.

Part One

Esther

Chapter One

Esther Campbell was in a foul mood. Walking next to her, on her leash, was Pebbles, her mutt, panting in the record-breaking heat. And they weren't even at the end of June yet. Esther headed toward the cluster of food trucks stationed in the parking lot at the beach, seeking out her newest addiction, a grilled PBJ. The trucks had been a popular addition to the Lavender Bay business community, but luckily, the line wasn't that long at her destination, Tom and Angie's Coffee Club, as most of the crowd were over at Scoopalicious, the ice cream truck. As she waited her turn, she opened her portable dog water bottle and set it down for Pebbles, who lapped at it greedily. She placed her order with Melissa, the manager.

"It hasn't been this hot since 1945!" Melissa said as she placed the sandwich, cut on the diagonal, in a brown paper wrapper.

"Great," Esther mumbled. She loved sunshine and heat, but today she wasn't in the mood for it. The humidity was so high her shorts and sleeveless T-shirt clung to her. She was grateful for her pixie haircut; she didn't know how those with long hair managed it. Even the thought of it made her sweat.

She stepped aside to let the next customer order and stood out of the way as she bit into her grilled PBJ. Who would have thought a different take on a childhood favorite could bring so much comfort. Pebbles looked up at her.

"Don't look at me like that," she said. Her dog was average in almost every way: brown in color with some black and some white, of average height and weight, basically unremarkable except for the way she had of curling her lip as if she were passing judgment. As she was doing at that very moment.

"Only my dog could make me feel like I'm a major disappointment," she muttered. To Pebbles, she said, "Yes, I know I had one yesterday, but I like them." The dog's lip remained curled. All she needed was to lift a shaggy eyebrow to complete the picture. Esther ate the rest of the sandwich, wiping her fingertips on the wrapper before tossing it into the trash. "Come on, I'll get you a pup cup."

In response, Pebbles wagged her tail and trotted happily at Esther's side over to the ice cream truck.

Three people stood in line ahead of Esther. Directly in front of her was one of the town's elder residents, Edith Bermingham, or Mrs. B as she was called, looking cool in a cream linen outfit. She turned toward Esther, her face shrouded by a wide-brimmed hat and a pair of oversized sunglasses.

"Hello, Esther. Hello, Pebbles."

The dog wagged her tail.

"Hello, Mrs. B, how are you?" Esther said.

"Wonderful. Enjoying the beautiful weather."

"I'm sweating," A drop fell from Esther's bangs, slid down her nose, and fell off like a jump off a ski slope. She swiped at her nose and forehead with her arm.

"Esther, men sweat. Women perspire," Mrs. B said quietly.

"That may be, but about an hour ago, I graduated from perspiring to sweating," Esther told her.

"How unfortunate."

"Exactly."

"My turn. It was nice to see you, Esther." Mrs. B approached the window and placed her order.

When it was Esther's turn, she ordered a pup cup and as much as she'd like an ice cream cone herself, the grilled PBJ had left her stuffed. Once she had her order, she walked over to the other end of the parking lot, nearest to Pearl Street, and settled herself beneath a shady oak tree, setting the cup down on the grass for the dog.

The shade did little to cool her or temper her mood. She'd taken the day off to spend with her sister, as she did from time to time. But Suzanne had canceled at the last minute, and here Esther was with a day off and nothing to do.

"Come on, let's go see Grandma," she said to Pebbles. "Maybe she'll have some words of wisdom."

She took the shortest route to her mother's antique shop, Prime Vintage, taking Pearl to Willow and then heading east until she reached Main Street, where the shop was located, right in the center of town.

The front door was wide open, and the interior of the shop was dark and cool with the sound of rotating metal blades from antique fans filling the space. There was one small desk lamp on at the back counter, where her mother's head was bent, her task laid out before her. The rest of the shop was darkened. Not one of the overhead chandeliers was turned on. It was probably what kept the space cool. Gail looked up and smiled when she spotted Esther and Pebbles.

"Hello there." Gail removed her glasses and let them dangle from the lanyard around her neck.

"Hey, Mom," Esther grumbled.

In the middle of the shop, on his back on a red settee, lay Gail's bloodhound, Rufus, snoring, seemingly oblivious to the stifling heat. Pebbles jumped up onto the other end of the settee, sniffed at Rufus's feet in the air, and settled in the corner.

Gail came out from behind the counter. "What's the matter?" she asked as she neared her daughter.

"Why do you think something's wrong?" Esther huffed.

"I don't know, maybe it was the black thundercloud that followed you into the shop," her mother said. She pulled over two antique embroidered chairs and said, "Sit down."

Esther took a chair from her mother and plopped down on it.

"Weren't you and Suzanne supposed to do something today? Have a girl's day out?" Gail asked.

"Yes, we were," Esther barked. "But she canceled at the last minute. This is the third time in the last two months."

Her mother rolled her lips inward but offered no comment. This fueled Esther's annoyance. "You know it's him," she said, referring to Suzanne's husband, Ray. "He says 'jump,' and Suzanne says 'how high.'"

"That's not fair," Gail said quietly.

"Isn't it? It's true."

Gail narrowed her eyes. "Why is this bothering you all of the sudden? This is not a new development in your sister's behavior. Or Ray's, for that matter."

"Why don't you try to talk to her?" Esther said.

Gail put out her hands, palms up, as if to say *What can I do?* "I tried talking to her years ago and finally decided it wasn't worth it if it was going to affect my relationship with my daughter and grandchildren." She narrowed her eyes at her oldest daughter. "Are you sure your bad mood doesn't have more to do with Lou?"

"I don't know," Esther grumbled.

Esther had been going out with Lou for a while, and she'd been happy. But he'd wanted to move in together and Esther hadn't wanted that kind of commitment. Although she'd broken it off with him months ago, she still missed him. She hated to admit it.

"It's quite possible your anger is a symptom of something related to Lou and you're transferring it to your sister," Gail said knowingly.

Esther rolled her eyes. "What kind of psychobabble is this, Mom?" she demanded. "Just because you've seen every episode of *Dr. Phil* doesn't mean you're a licensed psychologist."

Her mother shrugged. "Maybe not. But since you broke up with Lou, you've been a little off."

Esther scowled. "I have not."

Gail lifted her eyebrows and tilted her head slightly. "Really?"

"Why couldn't we stay as we were?" Esther asked. It was a rhetorical question, but it was one she'd asked Lou and herself over and over again. They'd been having a good time; why did he have to go and ruin things by suggesting they move in together? She'd been happy with the way things were. Besides, she'd never lived with anyone since moving out of her mother's house. She knew herself to be a solitary creature.

"Why can't you take that next step with Lou?" Gail asked.

"Why do I have to?" Esther snapped.

"I'm going to say something you're not going to want to hear," Gail prefaced. "All your romantic entanglements are superficial. You never want any of your relationships to get serious."

Esther shrugged. "It suits me."

"It wasn't always like this," her mother noted. "There was a time—"

Esther interrupted her and said loudly, "No need to go back into the history books."

"All right, we'll leave it at that. Anything else you want to vent about?" Gail asked.

"Yes. The bowling alley last night was an inferno. The air conditioning was broken," Esther complained. "Even the balls were sweaty."

Her mother feigned outrage. "My goodness! How did you ever manage it? These first-world problems are really something else."

Esther put up a hand. "Okay, Mom."

Gail laughed. "Come on, where's your sense of humor?"

"I don't know. I've lost it along the way." Esther looked over at Pebbles, watching her chest rise and fall as she breathed deeply, fast asleep. Next to her, Rufus snored, unbothered, as Esther and Gail conversed right in front of him.

"I have some news," Gail said.

"Yes?" Esther could do without the dramatic pause.

"I heard from Rose last night."

"Really?"

Rose Campbell was Esther's cousin on her late father's side. She'd been born in Lavender Bay and went to school with Esther, but the family had moved to Florida. She was divorced now, and she and her children lived with her mother. She infrequently came back to Lavender Bay to visit and whenever Esther, Suzanne, and Gail traveled to Florida, they always made time to get together. But it had been two years since they'd seen them.

"When we were young, she was the most beautiful girl in Lavender Bay," Esther recalled.

"She was. But sometimes beauty is a curse. Her life hasn't been perfect."

Esther supposed not. "How are they?" she asked.

"They're all fine. Actually, Rose and her mother and kids are coming up for a visit. They asked if they could stay with me."

"Did she say when?"

Gail shook her head. "Nothing definite yet, but they'd like to see everyone."

"It'll be good to see them."

"Hopefully, you'll be in a better frame of mind by then."

"Here's hoping."

"Why don't you go home and go for a swim?"

"Maybe. Come on, Pebbles, let's go," Esther said. The dog snapped up her head and jumped off the settee. Esther clipped the leash back onto her collar.

Gail walked her out. As they neared the open front door, Esther could feel the day's heat. She dreaded the walk home.

"Cheer up, honey, it's not like you to be grumpy," Gail said.

"I can't be perfect all the time," Esther said, stepping out onto the sidewalk. Her mother's laughter rang in her ears as she walked away, heading in the direction of home. Her sour mood had left her feeling off-center and she didn't like it one bit.

Certainly, things would get better, wouldn't they?

Chapter Two

Esther left the antique shop feeling no satisfaction after her conversation. She'd expected her mother to side with her, to join her in her concern and annoyance with her sister and her less-than-stellar marriage. But apparently, her mother had given up, which surprised her. Gail Campbell was one to not only have strong opinions but to voice them as well, never shy about giving advice, unsolicited or otherwise.

Although Esther had the day off from her remote job as an IT support worker, she thought she might do some work on her side gig, which she should really attend to. She loved working from home; she found it freeing, and although there was a lack of social interaction with coworkers, she felt she had that covered with her nights out bowling and seeing her extended family.

Despite the unrelenting heat, she picked up her pace. She had one more stop to make, at the Quirk and the Quill, just down the street from her mother's shop. She looked both ways, encouraged Pebbles to hurry up, and crossed the street. The Quirk and the Quill was Lavender Bay's only stationery shop, and it had been there for as long as Esther could remember.

She found a shady spot beneath a large oak tree in front of the shop and tied Pebbles's leash to the grate. She set down her water bottle and opened it for her. "I won't be long," she promised.

After the bowling alley, this was one of Esther's favorite places in town. The elderly owner, Loretta Young Jablonski, had opened the Quirk and the Quill more than fifty years ago, and it had been supplying the paper-and-pen needs of the town ever since. Esther had no idea how she stayed open during these times of online shopping and big box office supply stores but every time she went in, there were always customers inside. It couldn't hurt that Loretta had the best selection of greeting cards in town.

Mrs. Jablonski was easy to spot with her dyed red hair. She stood at the counter talking to another lifelong resident of Lavender Bay, Edna Knickerbocker. Esther approached them. "Good morning, ladies," she said with a smile.

Behind the counter, Mrs. Jablonski smiled back. Edna turned and said, "And a good morning to you too."

"You two look like you're conspiring," Esther teased.

"Not at all," Edna said, her voice serious.

"She was telling me about some of her home remedies," Mrs. Jablonski chimed in.

Esther turned her attention back to Mrs. Knickerbocker. "And what would they be?"

"A shot of whiskey for just about everything," Edna said. "A headache, an upset stomach, depression, anxiety, and especially for sisters who get on your nerves."

Mrs. Jablonski laughed, well aware of Edna's decades-long feud with her sister, Edith Bermingham.

"I'd need a whole bottle for my sister," Esther said.

Mrs. Knickerbocker added, "Remember, dear, you choose your friends, not your relatives."

"Isn't that the truth."

"Now, I must get going. Hal and I are going strawberry picking," Edna said, referring to her next-door neighbor. "Ta-ta."

"Bye, Mrs. Knickerbocker."

"Talk to you later, Edna." Mrs. Jablonski stepped out from behind the counter, carrying a roll of paper towels and a bottle of window cleaner. She began to wipe down the glass shelves. She still wore her nice-sized wedding set on her left hand, even though she'd been widowed for years.

"How are you, Mrs. Jablonski?" Esther asked.

"I'm well, Esther. How are you?"

"I'm good," Esther lied. No sense in spreading her less-than-cheerful mood around. "What's new with you?"

Mrs. Jablonski shook her head. "Nothing. Same thing, different day."

"Sometimes that's not a bad thing," Esther said. "There's security in routine."

"I guess so," the older woman said with a sigh. "Are you here for your birthday cards?"

"I am," Esther said. There were two birthdays this month: her nephew Patrick and her cousin Maureen's husband, Allan. She didn't take too long, conscious of the dog sitting outside under the tree. She picked two cards, cashed out, and went back out into the bright daylight. Pebbles was sound asleep beneath the tree, her front paws crossed. Her water bottle remained undisturbed next to her.

Gently she woke the dog, who jumped up, wagging her tail. Esther laughed. Her dog always made her smile; she was always so agreeable. She had to get a hold of her playbook.

"Come on, Pebbles, let's go home," she said.

As she walked, multiple thoughts coursed through her mind. The first was Lou. They'd been together awhile, ever since she'd met him at the hot air balloon festival more than two years ago. She liked his company. They shared the same interests, and he had a great sense of humor. She debated texting him, asking for a meet-up to see if there might be room for a compromise. But immediately her pride stepped in and held her back. Lou had made it very clear that he wanted to go forward and wouldn't settle for less. And Esther had made it very clear that permanency was not in the cards for her.

Sighing, she switched her focus to her sister. There was nothing new about Suzanne's relationship with her husband. This was how it had always been. He was a control freak, and her sister put up with it. But why did it bother her now? After all this time? Possibly because there'd been too many cancellations in a row? Or maybe her mother was right; maybe it bothered her more now because she was viewing it through the lens of the loss of Lou. She was still hurting from the breakup and she was in need of her sister's support. But how could she when she was constantly a no-show? Maybe deep down, she was hurt and feeling abandoned.

Louise Cook, Esther's aunt, had a full house the following Sunday morning for her weekly coffee gathering. Esther was the first to arrive, carrying in two bags of coffee: one blueberry-flavored, the other orange. She'd taken a drive up to Cheever the day before and stopped at a specialty coffee shop and picked up a few bags. It was a place Lou had frequently taken her to.

"Thanks," Louise said, taking the coffee from her. "I already have regular coffee in the coffeemaker, but we can use the stovetop percolator."

Esther nodded. She went over to the stove and took the lid off the percolator, then took the scissors her aunt handed her and cut open the first bag of coffee, closing her eyes and sighing as she inhaled the scent. She took a dessert spoon out of the drawer and began scooping coffee out of the bag and into the metal basket. After she filled the pot with water, she assembled everything and put it on the stove, turning on the burner.

Louise's rescue cat, Peter, was curled up in the corner of the kitchen. Partially blind and with only three legs, they could only guess at the difficulties he'd experienced in the past. He regarded Esther with his one good eye.

"How's it going with Peter?" Esther asked.

Louise looked over at him and smiled. "He's a sweetheart! God bless him, but despite his infirmities, he makes the best of it."

Esther smiled at the cat, thinking he'd hit the jackpot finding a home here with Louise. She was sure there was a lot of spoiling going on. There was something so satisfying about an animal that had suffered finally finding a good, loving home.

Everyone began to trickle in and as soon as it became apparent that there were more people than usual, Esther went to the spare room and helped Maureen bring out a card table and a couple of folding chairs. As they set the card table up as an extension of the farmhouse table, Louise said, "It's a good thing we put on that extra pot of coffee."

Maureen and Allan had brought along their young adult sons, Everett and Lance. Esther talked to Lance about installing a ceiling fan beneath the canopy of her backyard patio. He promised to stop over within the next week.

Esther's cousin DeeDee approached, and Esther hugged her. "How are you? How are things going over at the community theater?" she asked.

"They're going great. Auditions and rehearsals for our next production will be starting up soon. I've got all kinds of workshops and mini master courses planned for the members of the theater group. Are you interested?" DeeDee asked with a smile and an arched eyebrow.

Esther put up her hands and laughed. "No way. I was a one-hit wonder!" she said, referring to her role in the play DeeDee had written for the hundredth birthday of the theater's patron and namesake, Grace Gibson.

DeeDee's sister Angie arrived with her partner, Tom Sloane, and his brother, Jim, who owned a tattoo place in town called the Ink Stain. Jim had done Esther's tattoo of a butterfly on her ankle. Debbie Melvin, Angie's best friend since grade school, arrived with a dozen donuts, her bright red hair piled high as usual in a messy updo. Upon spotting Debbie, Peter the cat stood up in his bed on his three legs and stared at her until she went to him and showered him with affection and told him how well he looked.

Suzanne came in with her older daughter, Sophie, and her two young sons, Patrick and Jason, and everyone made a fuss over them. Suzanne sat with her boys and her mother down at one end of the table. Esther took a place at the other end, sitting with Angie, Tom, Jim, and Debbie. Her fifteen-year-old niece took the chair next to her.

"I'm surprised to see you here. You're always with your friend Julia," Esther said to Sophie. Teenagers usually had better things to do than hang out with their grandmothers and aunts.

Sophie rested her chin on her hand. "Julia has a boyfriend and appears to have forgotten my name."

"Oh boy," Esther said sympathetically.

Coffee mugs were passed around, and the coffeepots were set on trivets at the table. There were platters of donuts and pastry hearts. Esther fixed her coffee with cream and sugar and stirred it with a spoon.

"How's everything over at the Ink Stain?" she asked Jim.

Jim nodded. "Good. Busy."

Esther nodded. "That's the way to be."

"Any rescues this week?" Esther asked Debbie.

Debbie's big gold hoop earrings swayed as she nodded enthusiastically. "Yes!"

Out of the corner of her eye, Esther noticed that Jim's attention was fixed on Debbie. He was rapt. Debbie was oblivious. Esther smiled to herself. *The course of true love never runs smooth.*

Debbie went on. "Another cat. People really need to get their pets neutered. My house seems to be a revolving door for cats."

Esther knew Debbie didn't mind. She lived for this sort of thing.

"Anyway," Debbie said, "he's an older cat. Almost ten years old. His owner died"—here she grimaced—"and none of the family could take him. It's very sad. He probably doesn't know what's going on, the poor thing."

"He might be easier to rehome, being an older cat," Angie said.

Debbie shook her head. "Unfortunately, no. Everyone wants the cute kittens. Besides, Timmy has some strange habits."

"Timmy?" Jim asked.

Debbie nodded. "That's right. That's his name."

"What kind of strange habits?" Tom asked, drinking from his coffee mug.

"He likes to close the blinds."

They all stared at Debbie, speechless, until Esther asked, "What do you mean?"

"He sits on the back of the couch and uses his paw to close the slats of the venetian blinds," she explained. "I open them up and he goes over and closes them. We go through this every day. All day. I wouldn't mind it at night, but I like all the drapes and windows open during the day." Debbie's fear of windowless rooms was no secret.

"That doesn't sound too bad," Tom said.

"Can we get another cat to keep Mr. Beans company?" Angie asked enthusiastically.

"No," Tom said firmly. "Mr. Beans has enough bad habits of his own. We don't need him teaching Timmy, or whatever his name is, any more."

"Aw," Angie said, drawing the word out for effect.

"What about you, Jim?" Debbie asked.

"Huh?" he asked as if he hadn't been paying attention.

If he'd stop looking at Debbie with hearts in his eyes, Esther thought, he could keep track of the conversation.

"Do you have room in your heart and home for Timmy?" Debbie asked.

"Be careful, brother, this is how she reels you in," Tom said with a laugh.

Jim stuttered, "Um, well, you see—"

Debbie cut him off. "I'll bring him over so you can meet him."

And Jim, who tended to give off a bad-boy vibe with his well-muscled body and the tattoos covering his arms, was apparently putty as far as Debbie Melvin was concerned. With an uncertain grin, he replied, "That's great."

Debbie nodded, satisfied.

Tom shook his head as if to say his younger brother was a lost cause.

Gail walked down from the other end of the table, carrying her coffee cup. "This orange coffee is wonderful."

"I thought so too," Esther said.

Gail took a seat next to her. "I wanted to let you know that I heard from Rose last night. They'll be here in two weeks."

"How old are Rose's children now?" Esther asked.

"Becky is fifteen and Connor is nine or ten."

Esther nodded.

Next to them, Angie asked, "Is her mother coming as well?"

Gail nodded and helped herself to a pastry heart. "I always liked Lydia, but she used to be terribly shy, especially when I was first married to Hugh and she was married to his brother," Gail said. "She never said boo."

Grinning, Esther said, "There's probably two reasons for that, Mom: first, you never stop talking and second, you're a larger-than-life personality. She might have been overwhelmed."

Gail shrugged, laughing. "Maybe, maybe not."

Angie leaned into her aunt. "I love that Aunt Gail is larger than life!"

"Thank you, sweetie," Gail said.

"How long are they staying?" Esther asked.

"She didn't say."

"Didn't you ask?" Esther said.

Her mother frowned. "Of course not. That would be rude."

"It'll be nice to see someone from Hugh's family," Louise declared. "It's important to keep in touch."

"That's how I feel," Gail said. "She always sends me a card at Christmas with a note in it. No one really sends out cards anymore. I only get a handful now every year."

"It's a shame. That was always a wonderful tradition," Louise said. "But with all this technology, it's fallen by the wayside."

There was a joint put-upon sigh between Gail and Louise, lamenting an almost-extinct tradition.

That would be one good thing about the summer, Esther thought: Rose's arrival. She'd make sure to spend some time with her and Aunt Lydia and the kids. She'd invite them over to enjoy the pool—all kids liked swimming in hot weather. She wondered if they liked bowling.

Chapter Three

Esther spent the next afternoon huddled over her laptop at her kitchen table with the air conditioning cranked up high. She purposefully avoided looking out the window. The brilliant sunshine made her wish she were outside in her pool, but there was work to be done.

Pebbles was sound asleep in her dog bed, and curled in next to her were Esther's two rescue cats, courtesy of Debbie Melvin: Billy Bojangles and Sylvia.

Once her IT work was finished, Esther turned her attention to her side gig, something she'd stumbled into while looking to occupy some of her free time after she'd broken things off with Lou. She'd set herself up as a professional apology writer, surprising herself by finding she had a knack for it. Today there were three apologies to be written. She tackled the easiest one first. Some guy had canceled a date two times in a row for legitimate reasons, but the person of interest didn't believe him.

Although the relationship had crashed and burned before it even got off the ground, he wanted to send a decent apology letter to the young woman. Esther could do decent. She felt like writing to the woman herself and telling her to hang on to this one.

In their limited emails back and forth, Esther had gathered information from the man, trying to get a sense of him so she could personalize his apology. She'd told him she'd have it back to him within two days.

It took her all of fifteen minutes to pen the letter, using a rough template she'd developed and filling it in with the details the client had given her.

Dear Sarah,

I want to apologize for canceling our date a second time, both due to unforeseen circumstances beyond my control. I realize your opinion of me must be at a low point and I can't say I blame you. I deeply regret being unable to meet up with you.

I can only imagine how frustrating and disappointing it must have been when I had to cancel at the last minute. Twice. That was never my intention, and I am truly sorry for letting you down.

I take full responsibility for my actions. I won't bore you with the reasons, but please accept my apology.

I hope you can find it in your heart to forgive me and most of all, give me a second chance—well, a third chance.

I was really looking forward to our date and getting to know you better.

I'll understand if you want nothing further to do with me. I'm a strong believer in the idea that actions have consequences.

Sincerely,

Justin

Satisfied, Esther emailed the client the text for feedback and advised him to send the woman flowers as well if he was truly serious about trying to meet up with her. Not roses, she advised, but a mixed colorful bouquet instead.

The remaining two were just as easy. She wrote and rewrote them until she was happy with the results.

Now that all her work commitments were finished, she could concentrate on her passion project: the bowling camp. It was something she and Lou had brainstormed about, but she'd finally taken steps on her own to make it happen. This summer would be the inaugural year for her bowling camp for kids eight to fourteen. When her registration numbers reached twenty kids, she'd crowed with delight, although her enthusiasm had been tempered by the fact that she was unable to share this good news with Lou. The camp's duration was two weeks and the kids would be there every morning, Monday through Friday, from nine until noon. Esther would use two weeks of her vacation time to run it. It was going to be great fun. She had everything planned out, including a party on the last day. Assuming the summer camp went well, she planned to approach the high school about starting an after-school bowling club. Bowling was her passion, and nothing gave her greater satisfaction than passing on that love of the sport to others, especially younger people.

She looked over the roster of youngsters, grouping them by ages, counting not once but twice, happy to see there were now twenty-five sign-ups for this summer. They were going to have a great time.

There was a knock at her door, it opened, and a voice called out, "Aunt Esther?"

"Come on in, Sophie," Esther said.

She put aside the camp paperwork and stood from the table. Pebbles jumped out of her bed, disturbing the cats, and ran to the teenaged girl.

"Hello, Pebbly poo," Sophie cooed. The cats lifted their heads, decided there was no need to run away, and repositioned themselves in the dog bed, laying their heads down and closing their eyes.

"What brings you here?" Esther said.

Sophie was the image of her mother: the same lithe build, the long sandy-brown hair, and the sharp eyes. She was Suzanne Jr.

Sophie plopped onto the sofa, and Pebbles jumped up and curled up next to her.

"Ugh. Mom is treating me like I'm a rented mule or something," Sophie said with an exaggerated sense of disdain. "I mean, come on, it's my summer vacation. Finally get a break from school and she expects me to do housework." Her eyes grew larger as she said, "Like, all the time!"

Esther sat in the chair across from the sofa and crossed her legs. "Yeah, that'd be a drag. It doesn't get any better when you get older, I hate to tell you."

Sophie made a face of disgust.

"Where's Julia today?" Esther asked.

Sophie crossed her arms over her chest and rolled her eyes. "Take a guess?"

Esther cast a sympathetic glance at her niece. "With the boyfriend?"

A floodgate opened and her niece ranted, "I hardly ever see her anymore and when I do, all she can talk about is Jamie. Jamie this and Jamie that. Give it a rest."

"What about you? Are you dating anyone?" Esther asked

"How can I when I'm home dusting and vacuuming all the time?" Sophie asked.

"How long has she been going out with Jamie?"

"Since winter break. I thought it would be over by now," Sophie said, rolling her eyes.

"Don't you like him?"

Sophie tilted her head slightly and narrowed her eyes. "He's all right."

Esther nodded, and Sophie continued. "What infuriates me is she makes plans with me and then as soon as Jamie calls, she drops me. I'm like, um, hello? I'm your best friend?"

Esther didn't miss the indignation in her niece's voice. "That isn't right," she said.

"No, it isn't."

"This scenario has played out for generations."

Sophie frowned. "What do you mean?"

"This happens. Girls are best friends and as soon as one gets a boyfriend, the other girl is forgotten or shoved aside. It happened when I was your age and unfortunately, I've done it to my friends." She was certain there had been times when she'd dropped her friends when she started going out with her old boyfriend Derrick. "And I'm sure your grandmother and Aunt Louise have some experience with it."

Her niece scrunched up her face. "It's hard to picture Grammy dating."

Esther laughed. "Don't picture it. But we wouldn't be here if she hadn't gone out with someone."

For whatever reason, Sophie found this funny and burst into giggles.

"Yeah, like I said, don't picture it." Esther was glad to see her niece lightening up. "Anyway, Julia is only fifteen. This is puppy love. It will run its course and she'll be back to you in no time." She paused, reflective, and added, "And who knows, by then you might have a boyfriend yourself."

"Even if I do, I won't break my plans with my friends to be with him."

Here's hoping, Esther thought. "You know what I think you need? What would cheer you up?"

Sophie looked at her aunt with uncertainty. "I don't know, what?"

"Why don't we go over to the alley and bowl a few games?"

Sophie laughed. "Aunt Esther, is bowling the solution to everything?"

Esther didn't have to think about it. "Yes."

She managed to twist Sophie's arm, and they went over to the bowling alley and bowled two games. Afterward, Esther treated her niece to a cone at the Scoopalicious ice cream truck at the beach and then drove her home. As Sophie got out of the car, Esther leaned over and said, "And don't worry about Julia, she'll find her way back to you." Or at least Esther hoped she would.

Chapter Four

A week later, Esther was out early with Pebbles. It was only the first of July, and it was starting off as a scorcher of a summer. The forecast for the day was mid-nineties, so it would be too hot to walk in the afternoon. She loved walking around town at six thirty in the morning. Everything was still and quiet. There was hardly any traffic, and everything was blanketed in a warm, sleepy vibe. When she walked past the bowling alley, she lifted two fingers to her forehead in a salute.

Suzanne had changed their plans. Again. They were to meet up the day before for lunch, but she'd rescheduled for the following week. Esther hadn't bothered to reply to her text. She'd been livid.

As she rounded the corner from Thistle onto Vine, now heading in the direction of home, she was so lost in thought that she forgot about the raised edge of the sidewalk. She tripped and sailed right into the chest of an unsuspecting man, dragging Pebbles along with her.

A pair of strong hands reached out to steady her.

"I am so sorry," Esther said, her face reddening. How embarrassing was this?

She didn't know what surprised her more: the fact that she'd tripped or the fact that there was someone else out on the streets this early in the morning and she'd landed right on them. The chest in front of her was broad and muscular, and there was a faint scent of Gray Flannel, which reminded her of something from her past.

"Esther? Esther Campbell?"

Recognizing the voice, she looked up and froze.

Derrick. Derrick Radich. Former boyfriend. The love of her life.

She hadn't seen him in more than two decades. She blinked several times in succession, not quite believing that he was standing in front of her. "Derrick!"

"I can't believe this! You literally ran right into me!" He hadn't changed much. His blond hair had gotten darker, and there was a liberal amount of gray at the sides. The cleft in his chin was still as fascinating as ever. He was all smiles.

The last time she'd seen him was the week before Christmas almost twenty-five years ago, when her anticipation for an engagement ring had been at an all-time high and instead, he'd told her he didn't want to see her anymore. That he was leaving Lavender Bay to go work for his uncle down in Florida. He'd admitted that he wasn't ready to settle down and that he wanted to "live a little." And what had she done? She'd cried and pleaded, told him how much she loved him, even offered to go with him. Looking back, she'd often thought that the job offer was his get-out-of-jail-free card. A year after he left her, he'd married someone else.

She swallowed hard. "What are you doing here?"

He laughed, the fine lines around his eyes deepening. "Here on Vine Street or here in Lavender Bay?"

"Lavender Bay." Over the years, she'd heard at times that he was home visiting his parents and during those visits, she'd kept a low profile until she was sure he was gone. If she had enough notice, she sometimes went out of town for a few days.

"My dad passed away six months ago, so I'm here to look after a few things," he said.

She nodded. "Mom showed me the obituary in *The Lavender Bay Chronicles*." Derrick's mother had passed away years ago; her mother had shown her that death notice as well.

"I thought you might come to the wake," he said quietly.

She shook her head. "It wasn't my place. That was a private affair."

"My parents always liked you."

"And I was fond of them." Sometimes, she'd run into them in places like the grocery store, and she was always polite, but it was painful for her. She was always left with the feeling that they could have been her in-laws. "Besides, I'm sure your wife wouldn't have appreciated my presence."

He looked down at the sidewalk before lifting his head again. "I'm divorced."

"I'm sorry about that," she mumbled. Was she really sorry? Or was it the polite thing to say?

He brushed it off with a shrug. There was an awkward pause, and she asked, "Do you have children?"

The expression on his face transformed into one of pure pride. "I have a son." He paused, looked around, and said, "Anyway, I'm home to wrap up my dad's estate. I've got to put the house on the market."

"You'll be busy," she said.

"You look great, Esther. You're as beautiful as I remember."

The resulting blush on Esther's face was so intense it could have set something on fire. He used to say that to her all the time when they were together.

"I've thought about you a lot over the years," he said.

She didn't know what to say. "Um, okay."

"Are you with someone?" he asked.

Caught off guard, she stammered, "Um, yes. No. Not really at the moment."

He laughed again. Laughing always came easy to him; it was one of the first things that had attracted her to him.

"I'm going to be in town for a few more weeks. Would you like to grab a coffee sometime and catch up?" he asked, slipping his hands into the pockets of his shorts and rocking back and forth on his heels.

What's the harm in catching up? Trying to play it cool, she said, "Sure."

He whipped out his phone, asked for her number, and added it to his contact list. There was a beep on her own phone.

Shoving his phone back into his pocket, he said, "I've sent you a text so you have my number too."

"Okay," she said with a nod. She looked down at Pebbles. "I'd better go."

"Sure. I'll call you."

"It was good to see you, Derrick."

"It was *great* seeing you, Esther."

Smiling, she side-stepped him and headed toward home with Pebbles at her side, her emotions conflicted. The lift in her mood was tempered by a sense of nervousness, as if she was about to row into uncharted territory.

Esther glanced at the clock, anxious to finish this one apology, if only the person who'd requested it would stop emailing her. She had to be somewhere. Her thoughts were all jumbled. All day she'd replayed the encounter with Derrick, not quite believing that she'd run into him after all this time and not quite sure how she felt about it. Some long-buried feelings had been disturbed and had risen to the surface. She turned her attention back to the apology at hand.

It had been a tough one to write, and she was pretty certain the outcome was preordained. A woman named Terry had been convicted of embezzling from her employer, who also happened to be her sister and brother-in-law. It was a court-ordered apology to go along with restitution. Esther sighed over this one. Despite the apology, the relationship was most likely damaged beyond repair. But she'd write it, and at least that would be done.

Dear Susie and Ron,
I want to sincerely apologize for all the hurt I've caused you. You were gracious enough to give me a job when I needed one and I repaid you with betrayal. My regret knows no bounds.

I can't begin to imagine all the pain I've caused. My only hope is that one day you might be able to forgive me.

I take full responsibility for my actions, which were egregious and disloyal. This is an unreserved apology.

I hope someday we can rebuild the bridge that I burned down.

Sincerely,
Terry

Terry promptly emailed Esther back to tweak some things. She wanted the word "betrayal" dropped. No sense in making it front and center, she explained. Although to Esther, who'd looked up the case online, stealing over half a million dollars from your sister already made it front and center. And Terry didn't understand the term "unreserved apology." Could that set her up for a lawsuit? Esther rolled her eyes at that one. And finally, she wanted the last line to be changed to *I hope someday we can rebuild the bridge between us.* Esther wanted to ask her if she really wanted her sister back in her life. It sounded to her like Terry wasn't fully engaged with her wrongdoing. Esther responded with some unsolicited advice and then told Terry she was welcome to tweak the apology as she saw fit. She did not hear back from her again.

Quickly, she turned off her laptop and fed the dog and the cats. She had to get to her mother's house for dinner.

She'd been invited along with Suzanne, Ray, and their kids. She was glad the kids were going to be there as they could serve as a buffer between her and her sister. And as far as she was concerned, Ray could stay home. Before the night was over, she'd be aggravated for sure.

Chapter Five

Gail had told Esther that she had a small twelve-pound turkey in the freezer that had to be cooked as she didn't want to throw it out. It would be like a mini-Thanksgiving dinner in July. Esther arrived with two cans of cranberry sauce and put them in the fridge. She'd just closed the fridge door when Suzanne arrived with Ray and the two youngest of their four children in tow. Patrick and Jason were eleven and seven, and both looked like their father, who was tall and thin with brown hair and brown eyes. Esther always thought those looks worked better on the kids. She hugged them both and asked them what was new in their lives. They were currently up to their eyeballs in baseball.

"Hey, Esther, how are you?" Ray said, and then he said no more. That was one of the things with her brother-in-law: He hardly ever spoke. Once you got past the polite necessities, it was total silence as if he had nothing to add to any conversation. It irritated Esther to no end.

"Where are Sophie and Margret?" Esther asked of her nieces, Margret being younger than Sophie at thirteen.

"They went to their friend's cottage in Canada for the weekend," Suzanne explained. "Didn't you get my text the other night?"

"Oh, I forgot about it," Esther said, not meeting her gaze.

"You're not mad because I canceled the other day, are you?" her sister asked.

"You seem to be canceling a lot lately," Esther said, and she shot a look over to Ray, who was helping Gail remove the turkey from the oven.

"Things happen," Suzanne said tightly. "I have four kids who are involved in a lot of activities."

Esther shrugged. "Then you're busy, I guess." Snarkily, she added, "I have a schedule too. Just because I don't have kids doesn't mean I'm not busy."

"I never said you weren't busy!" Suzanne snapped.

Esther turned her back on her sister and made small talk with her nephews.

Despite the already-arctic temperature of their mother's home—Gail loved the air conditioning on high—a frosty chill descended over the room.

Not only was there turkey and box stuffing, but there were also mashed potatoes, green beans, carrots, sweet potato casserole, cranberry sauce, and an apple pie Gail had picked up from the grocery store.

Halfway through dinner, Ray looked over to his wife and said, "Babe, can you get me more gravy?" He held up the empty gravy boat.

Suzanne jumped up.

Esther couldn't help herself. "Ray, are your legs broken?"

Ray turned his attention to her, frowning. "Huh?"

Underneath the table, Gail kicked Esther in the shin.

"Ow," Esther whispered. She looked at Ray. "You've been in this family long enough that surely you must feel comfortable refilling the gravy boat yourself."

Another kick in the shin. Esther winced.

"I don't mind," Suzanne said through gritted teeth. She went to the stove and filled the gravy boat.

But I do, Esther thought.

Ray didn't answer her.

"If Suzanne doesn't mind, then it's not a problem," Gail said smoothly.

"No, I just don't understand why Ray can't get up and get it himself," Esther persisted.

"Esther," Suzanne said sharply.

"Suze doesn't mind," Ray said.

"No, I don't mind," Suzanne agreed.

"Drop it," Gail warned Esther.

So Esther dropped it, but it didn't change how she felt about her brother-in-law: she didn't like it one bit, the way he treated her sister. Like the maid.

Gail stood up abruptly and said, "I think it's time for pie."

A heavy silence settled over the table as they ate their dessert. Even the kids picked up on it. And by then, Esther wanted to kick herself. Why did she have to start something with the kids present? But she couldn't stand people treating other people unfairly.

"Ray, would you like more coffee?" Suzanne asked. She looked pointedly at her sister and said, "Is it okay if I ask my husband if he wants more coffee? And if he does, do I have your permission to pour it?"

"Come on, Suzanne," Esther huffed.

Ray shook his head and stood up from the table. He said to the boys, "Come on, you two, finish your pie. You've got baseball practice."

Both boys pushed back their chairs and made ready to leave.

"Hey, wait a minute," Suzanne said. "You know the rule. Carry your own plates over to the sink."

"Aw, Mom," protested Jason.

"That's all right," Gail said. "I'll get them."

"No, you won't, Mom, you've done enough," Suzanne said.

Esther, who usually liked to voice her own opinion, did not interfere with these domestic rules of her sister's. What she couldn't understand was that she waited on her husband hand and foot and yet expected her kids to do things for themselves. Talk about mixed messages. Esther said nothing but she did shake her head.

Grumbling, Patrick and Jason carried their empty plates over to the sink.

"Come here and give your grandmother a kiss goodbye," Gail commanded. The boys stood on each side of her and kissed her on the cheek. Gail laughed. "Have a great practice. When's your next game?"

"Tuesday night," Patrick answered.

"I'll be there. Front and center." She smiled at them. "Go on now, you don't want to be late for practice."

At the door, Ray lifted his hand. "Thanks for the dinner, Gail, it was delicious."

"Any time, Ray."

"Ready, Suze?"

"Coming." Suzanne turned to her mother and kissed her on the cheek. "Thanks, Mom, it was delicious."

Esther cleared the table. Once the dishwasher was loaded and the pots soaking, she said her goodbyes to Gail and headed out the door, fed up with her sister. She and her mother did not discuss Suzanne or Ray. By her mother's attitude, she suspected she did not want to talk about it.

Chapter Six

The following evening, after she'd taken Pebbles for a long walk, Esther changed into her bathing suit, thinking a swim might be in order, and headed outside to her enclosed backyard. Her built-in pool was her pride and joy. It took up most of the yard, but she didn't care; it meant she had less grass to cut. Over the years, she'd added an awning off the back of the house so there was somewhere shady to sit. In addition, she had a carpenter build her a bar out back, complete with stools. Her side job had allowed her to purchase summer furniture and beach towels. She grabbed a towel from the outside cabinet and threw it near the pool steps. Pebbles had followed her out and had opted for her bed under the awning, away from the descending sun.

Esther skimmed the pool and then dove in and did a few laps. Refreshed, she got out, dried off, and wrapped the towel around her waist. She stepped behind the bar, plugged in the blender, and made a pitcher of margaritas. She salted the rim of a glass and filled it. Margarita glass in hand, she planted herself in one of the lounge chairs by the pool. Despite the sinking sun, the air was still hot and heavy. She closed her eyes and listened to the relaxing, almost meditative sound of the pool filter.

Behind her, the sliding glass door opened. She'd been expecting her cousin Maureen, as she'd texted her when she first arrived home. She wanted to tell someone about her meeting with Derrick, and Suzanne was usually the first person she turned to, but obviously, that wasn't going to happen. Besides, would Suzanne even be available to listen?

"Hey there," Maureen said by way of greeting.

Without turning around, Esther lifted up her glass and said, "Greetings! There's a pitcher of margaritas behind the bar. Help yourself."

"I'll go for a swim first, if you don't mind," Maureen said.

"Not at all. Just got out myself."

"Gosh, it was a hot one today."

"It sure was," Esther agreed.

Maureen laid her cover-up and sunglasses on the chair next to Esther's. She pulled her auburn hair up and tied it in a ponytail. "Was I glad to hear from you today! A dip in the pool was exactly the thing I needed."

"Maureen, I've said it a million times, you can come over any time and use the pool. You know where I keep the spare key on the off chance that I may not be home."

Her cousin twisted her mouth in discomfort. Esther shook her head. Why she needed an invite was beyond her. Maureen was like a sister to her; they'd grown up together, and of all the cousins, Maureen was closest to her in age.

"Esther, when was the last time you were at the beach?"

"I'd have to think about that. Maybe ten years ago. Twelve? I tagged along with Suzanne and the kids. Against my will, I might add."

Maureen laughed. "I figured as much. Although I suppose with the pool, there's no need to go to the beach."

"That's exactly why I got the pool," Esther explained. "I'm not a fan of sand. It's hot, it's difficult to walk on, and it gets everywhere. Plus, with the pool you can see the bottom, so you don't have to play a guessing game about what you just stepped on or what swam over your feet."

Maureen laid her towel next to the steps and slipped into the pool, waving water away from her as she waded further in. "This feels wonderful!"

"Good." Esther stood up and refilled her glass and poured one for Maureen as well. She set it on the concrete at the edge of the pool. Her cousin swam up, rested her arms on the ledge, and took a sip. "Yum. It's a good thing I walked over."

"You walked over? In this heat?" Esther asked.

Maureen shrugged. "It's not that far. Besides, I've been slacking with my exercise lately."

"Too busy or not interested?" Esther asked.

"A little bit of both," Maureen admitted.

Esther wasn't a natural exerciser, but she thought it important to walk Pebbles every day. "I find in the summer, I have no appetite in the heat," she told Maureen. Funny, but the margaritas were sliding down with no problem.

Maureen stepped out of the pool, grabbed her beach towel and drink, and headed over toward Esther and plopped into the chair next to her. Her skin, dotted with beads of water, glistened in the early evening sun.

"What's new with you?" Maureen crossed one leg over the other.

Esther lifted her glass to her lips. "Funny you should ask."

Maureen lifted an eyebrow.

As casually as she could, Esther said, "You'll never believe who I ran into today."

Maureen grimaced. "Not that guy you went out with who farted like it was an Olympic sport?"

Esther burst out laughing. "No, thank goodness, not him." That had lasted all of two dates. The guy, though very nice, had a problem with gas. Lots of it. Esther thought she was going to have to wear a mask or hang car deodorizer off one of his belt loops.

"I don't know then, who?"

Esther lowered her voice, almost as if afraid that if she spoke too loud, the spell might be broken.

"Derrick."

"Derrick," Maureen repeated, her forehead creasing. Her eyes slowly widened and her eyebrows lifted. "Your Derrick?"

Esther nodded. It was funny to hear him referred to in that way when he'd never been hers and had an ex-wife and a son to prove it. It served as a stark reminder that she had never really been his either.

Maureen bounced up from her chair and put a finger up. "Hold that thought. I need another margarita." She nodded toward Esther's glass. "Want one?"

Esther shook her head. "No thanks, I'm good."

Maureen quickly returned with a full glass and settled into her chair. "Okay, tell me everything."

Esther wondered if she was making too big a deal about this. After all, her relationship with Derrick had happened almost twenty-five years ago. She gave her cousin the shortened version of their encounter, leaving out the part where he'd called her beautiful and ending with, "He asked me to go out for coffee, to catch up."

Maureen blinked slowly. "Oh boy. There's a lot to unpack here, Esther."

"Is there?" Esther wondered out loud. It was only coffee.

Maureen nodded slowly.

Esther drew in a deep breath and considered having another margarita, but decided she was too comfortable to get up and make a second pitcher.

"All right, a few things," Maureen started. "What do you think about all of this? His unexpected reappearance in your life?"

Esther couldn't help but smile. "I don't know. I don't know what it means."

"Does it have to mean anything? Could it simply be a random encounter?"

Leave it to Maureen to be sensible about it.

"You haven't seen him since you broke up with him, correct?" Maureen said.

"Yes, except he broke up with me," Esther clarified.

"How does all this make you feel?"

"I'm not sure," Esther admitted. A part of her felt giddy and excited, another part felt anxious, and a small voice told her to run.

"Do you think you'll meet him for coffee?"

"I think I will." Noting Maureen's worried expression, Esther added, "You know me, I love coffee."

"Be careful," Maureen advised.

"It's only dinner, not a marriage proposal." That off-the-cuff crack, given in light of her history with Derrick, caused her to sag in her chair. He'd been her first real love, and she'd mistakenly thought he felt the same way about her. The ensuing breakup had been so painful she'd never allowed herself to love that completely and deeply again. Trying to keep the irritation out of her voice, she said, "He's probably leaving town soon. He's only here to clean out his father's house."

"What about Lou?" Maureen probed gently.

Esther shrugged. There was something about that breakup that still smarted. She loved Lou's company and they got along so well it had come as quite a surprise to her that he couldn't be happy with the way things were. Looking down at her lap, she busied herself with pulling at a loose thread on her beach towel. "We couldn't agree on a future."

Maureen said nothing. Esther, in an effort to lighten the mood, joked, "It feels like a lot of high school drama."

"Yes, it does."

And if there was one thing Esther abhorred, it was drama.

Chapter Seven

For the next few days, Esther chose to maintain a positive outlook. Derrick had called and asked her to meet him for coffee, pushing any thoughts of her conflict with Suzanne to the back of her mind. She went out of her way for her clients at work and as soon as an apology request came in, she tackled it, the words flowing right out of her.

Not knowing what else to do with the nervous energy and excitement she was feeling in anticipation of her meeting with Derrick, she decided to go over to the lanes and bowl a few games. That always put her in the right frame of mind.

Historically, Lakeside Bowling Lanes was pretty quiet during the summer. The leagues didn't operate until the fall and then wrapped up with tournaments in late spring. She couldn't wait to get back to it. But this would do.

"Esther, how you doin'?" asked the owner, Lenny Bastich, as she arrived. Lenny had been there for as long as Esther could remember. He hadn't changed much, with the fringe of white hair circling his bald head and the buttons on his shirt stretched across his paunch. She was pretty sure he'd looked the same when she first came here when she'd joined the bowling league in high school. At Christmas, she always gave Lenny a bottle of Jameson, which she knew him to be particularly fond of.

"I'm hanging in there," she answered.

"The usual? Lane six?"

"Please, it's my lucky lane," she said.

He chuckled. "I know that, Esther. That's why I always try to save it for you."

"And that is much appreciated."

"All ready for bowling camp?" she asked.

Lenny shrugged. "What's there to get ready for?" He waved in the direction of the lanes and the balls. "Everything the kids need is there."

When Esther had first run the idea by him—a summer bowling camp for kids—he'd listened and scratched the back of his head as he was apt to do when he was deep in thought. She could practically see the dollar signs in his eyes. She'd assured him she'd take care of everything and all he had to do was provide the venue. It hadn't taken much convincing.

Briefly, she updated him on a few particulars, like how many kids had signed up and for what times. He'd nodded. Lenny Bastich had a mind like a steel trap. As she headed off to bowl, she told him she'd touch base with him right before the start of the camp.

The alley was mostly deserted. At the far end of the lanes was an elderly couple who Esther recognized. Like her, they were frequent bowlers. They spotted her and threw up their hands in a wave. Esther returned the gesture.

She reached her lane, kicked off her sandals, and pulled on a pair of socks and her bowling shoes. She set up her scorecard and removed her bowling ball from its case, then walked to the lane and threw the first ball, thinking, like she did every time she stepped onto the lane, how good it felt to throw it.

She couldn't explain her love of bowling. There were so many positives about it: the release of the ball, the rumble as it rolled down the lane, and that satisfying noise when it came in contact with the pins. She didn't understand why more people didn't take up the sport.

As she bowled, it was impossible to avoid thinking about Derrick. She tried to figure out the sway he had over her. Was it unfinished business? Lack of proper closure? Boy, how she hated that word. Or was it much simpler than that—was it because he was her first serious boyfriend, her true love? Was it because she felt like they had a connection, like they had all those years ago?

Her first game ended in a slight drop from her usual average. Determined to improve, she bowled a second and third game, satisfied that her score was finally coming up to where it should be. After three games, she called it a night, thinking she should get home and take Pebbles for one final walk before they went to bed.

The night air was warm, and the sky was dark with cloud cover. Hopefully there'd be some overnight rain to cool things down a bit. She was parked across the street and looked both ways before stepping off the curb. As she approached her car, she caught sight of Lou ahead of her, walking along, eating an ice cream cone. It was sure to be chocolate on a regular cone. He never deviated. There was a time, not too long ago, when she and Pebbles would have been walking along with him. Her heart ached at the sight of him. She missed him. That realization was startling.

If she'd hoped to get to her car unnoticed, she was sadly mistaken. Lou spotted her, changed direction, and walked over to her. She stepped onto the sidewalk so they wouldn't be standing in the middle of the street.

As she waited for him, she muttered to herself, "This is going to be all kinds of awkward."

Lou stood in front of her, ice cream cone in hand.

"How are you, Esther?" he asked quietly.

"Fine," she said. She tried to keep lightness in her voice. She knew he'd been hurt when she'd broken it off between them. She held up her bowling ball case and said, "Bowling always puts me in good spirits."

"I know," he said, taking a lick of his cone. He pivoted and threw the rest of it, along with his napkin, into a nearby sidewalk receptacle.

"How are you?" she asked.

"As good as can be expected."

Lou Gunderman was fifty-two. He had divorced when his sons were young and had been left to raise them alone. The boys were now grown men with families of their own and lived in other states. Although he wasn't conventionally handsome, Esther had always found him attractive. He was only a few inches taller than she, with a stocky body. He wore rimless glasses over his blue eyes. But it was his hair she'd always been intrigued by. Once dark, it was now gray with liberal streaks of white, and it had a beautiful wave. She missed touching it.

"How are the boys?" she asked. She'd met them a few times. Initially they'd seemed wary but once they got used to her being around, they'd warmed up to her. She'd even traveled with Lou out of state to visit them. She couldn't, however, convince them to go bowling when they came home to visit their father.

He sighed. "Good, but disappointed to hear that we . . ." His voice trailed off.

"Broke up?" she added. Was that the word? "Couldn't come to a compromise?" Although they'd never seen anyone else while they spent time together, they'd never actually said they were in a committed relationship, which was why it must have come as a surprise to Lou when she'd refused to move in with him.

His face remained impassive, his expression hard to read, even as they stood beneath the streetlight.

To alleviate the awkwardness that settled around them, she asked, "No fun facts for me, Lou?"

Lou was the king of trivia. The amount of knowledge he had stored in his brain was mind-boggling. They'd even joined a team for trivia night at Dog Days Bar when they were going out.

Without missing a beat—because he had all this information at his fingertips, like some sort of supercomputer—he said, "Fifty percent of all marriages end in divorce in the US."

Esther laughed nervously. "Cheery."

"I miss you, Es," he said. He was the only one in the world who called her that. Prior to meeting him, no one had ever shortened her name.

"I miss you too, Lou," she said truthfully. "But there's no sense to this as we've reached a stalemate."

"Thanks for reminding me," he said. "You don't want to make a commitment, and I do."

Grrr. It wasn't as simple as that, and she said as much. "Just because I don't want to move in with you doesn't mean that I wasn't committed."

"Look, Esther, I'm sorry I bothered you." He turned and walked away into the night.

She watched him go. He never looked over his shoulder. And the peace of mind she'd felt upon leaving the bowling alley evaporated, just like that.

CHAPTER EIGHT

Esther had fussed with her appearance, applying a bit of makeup and going for casual summer wear, trying to look natural and not as if she were trying too hard. It had been a long time since she'd been out with Derrick. As she walked out the door and assured her pets she wouldn't be long, she reminded herself, *It's only coffee. Only a catch-up.*

Derrick had suggested meeting at Coffee Girl on Main Street, but Esther had hesitated as her cousin Angie owned the place, and she knew that before she and Derrick even finished their first cup of coffee, the news of their meeting would spread through the family grapevine. Instead, she'd suggested they go to Java Joe's, which was right across the street. Whereas Coffee Girl was all about pastries and baked goods, Java Joe focused more on the savory side of things. But the coffee was good there too.

She walked into town from her home, thinking she'd like some fresh air to clear her head. She didn't want to appear overeager. However, the decision to walk turned out to be a poor one. The sun blazed overhead and by the time she reached Main Street, she was hot and sweaty. *Nice.*

It satisfied her to no end to see Derrick standing beneath the shade of the awning outside Java Joe's café. He was tanned, wearing khaki-colored Bermuda shorts, a yellow polo shirt, and a pair of boat shoes.

She threw her hand up in a wave and crossed the street to meet him.

"Hey there," he said. When he smiled, it lit up his whole face.

"I hope you weren't waiting long," she said.

"Not at all." He opened the door and indicated she should go in first. Esther removed her sunglasses and allowed her eyes to adjust to the change in the light inside. The blast of air conditioning was welcome.

They grabbed a table in the back corner and Esther did a quick scan of the café to see if there was anyone there that she knew. Of the relative sort.

"Hi, Esther!"

She turned and came face to face with Everett, Maureen's son, who held a bus pan full of dirty dishes. Tom, a.k.a. Java Joe, had given him a job when he desperately needed one and was coming out of his drug addiction.

"Hey, Everett," Esther said brightly. "How are you? How's college?"

"It's going well."

"I'm glad to hear that."

Everett's gaze swung over to Derrick, and Esther knew she'd have to introduce them. "Derrick, this is my cousin Maureen's oldest son, Everett. Everett, this is an old friend of mine, Derrick."

They nodded to each other and Esther said, "We better let you get back to work."

"Talk to you later, Esther," Everett said.

"For sure."

Derrick pulled out a chair for Esther and she sat. He took the chair next to her. It was odd sitting in a café with him. It had once been their norm.

The server, whose nametag read 'Loni', approached, handing them menus and listing off the specials of the day. Esther thought if she ate well, she wouldn't have to cook dinner later that evening.

Once Loni took their drink orders and left, Esther asked, "How are things going with your dad's estate?"

"Good. There's lots to do, but luckily, Dad kept meticulous records. He and Mom filled out one of those journals, literally titled *What to Do in the Event of My Death*."

Esther nodded. "Thoughtful and handy."

"It has made my life extremely easy."

Derrick leaned forward, resting tanned arms on the table. "The will has gone on into probate, and I've got a meeting with a realtor to sell the house."

"You haven't thought about keeping it?"

He shook his head. "No reason to. My life is in Florida now."

Inwardly, she flinched.

Loni returned to take their orders. The menus sat untouched on the table. "Do you need more time?" the server asked.

Derrick picked up the menu, opened it, and scanned it.

"I'll have an order of the taco fries," Esther said to the server.

The server nodded. "Anything else?"

"And a glass of unsweetened iced tea," Esther said.

Derrick snapped the menu shut. "I'll have the burger, no onions, and a side of the dirty fries. Can I get a Coke?"

"Sure."

While they waited for their meals, they fell into easy conversation. It was as if the years in-between had melted away and they'd only just seen each other the day before.

"Do you remember when we went to the Prince concert?" he asked.

"That was a long time ago. I think I was twenty," Esther said with a shake of her head. She hadn't thought of that in a long time.

"It was one of our first dates," he said.

"It was. You remember."

"Of course," he said in mock offense.

Loni arrived and set their drinks down in front of them. Both picked up their glasses at the same time and sipped.

"Do you still listen to Prince?" he asked.

"On occasion. My musical tastes haven't changed much. Still love pop and rock. How about you?"

He set his glass down and made a slight sucking sound with his lips, which slammed Esther back into the past. She'd forgotten this gesture of his.

"Actually, I've gone over to country," he said.

"No way!" She remembered him being a huge fan of rock and heavy metal. At the time, their musical tastes had intersected at rock.

He laughed. "I go to a lot of concerts." He leaned over and whispered, "I even have a cowboy hat and a pair of cowboy boots."

Esther bent her head and laughed. "It sounds like your transformation is complete."

"Almost. I go to Nashville a lot. Have you ever been there?"

"No, I haven't," she said.

"It's a great city. Vibrant."

Nashville wasn't on her short list of places she wanted to visit. She liked cruises and the islands.

Their meals were brought out and set in front of them. Esther's mouth watered at the sight of the taco fries. She picked up her fork, speared a fry, and popped it into her mouth.

They spoke about what they did for a living. She told him about her IT job, and he explained that he was a construction engineer. He also told her that he'd been divorced for years but wasn't currently dating anyone.

"Do you see your son often?" she asked. She supposed it was a prying question, but she was curious.

"I sure do. We're big Miami Dolphins fans. We have season tickets. Luckily, his mother and I are better friends than spouses."

"That's great."

"Bryce is eighteen now. He graduated from high school last month and doesn't know what he wants to do. I told him not to worry about it, that he's young yet and he'll figure it out."

"That sounds like good advice."

"So, he's working for me this summer and he's enrolled in the college down there. Going to take some general education courses."

Esther nodded, made sounds of approval, not sure what to say.

Derrick tucked into his burger. "Man, this is good."

They were quiet for a few moments, sitting in companionable silence as they ate their lunch.

"Remember that time we went out on the boat on the lake?" he said.

"The one you stole?" Esther asked with an arched eyebrow and a laugh.

"I didn't steal it," he said, laughing. "It belonged to my uncle, and I borrowed it."

"As I recall, uncle or not, he wanted to press charges," Esther teased.

"Luckily, my father talked him out of it."

"How did he do that?"

"He gave him an expensive bottle of whiskey."

They had a good laugh over that memory, and Derrick sighed and said, "That was a good night."

"It was." She remembered the stillness of the water and the moon bright over the lake. It had been perfect.

They finished up their meals and Esther went to pay the bill, but Derrick put up his hand and said, "No, this is on me."

After lunch, they strolled along Main Street until Esther decided it was time to go home.

"Can I see you again?" Derrick asked. "It's been fun reminiscing."

Esther nodded in agreement.

"Why don't we go to the beach?" he suggested. "It's supposed to be hot again tomorrow."

Of all places. "I can't tomorrow, I'm working."

"Want some company?" he asked.

She wasn't sure if he was joking or not. Since she'd started working from home, she'd discovered that some people equated remote work with being home and available for socializing.

"I'm afraid I wouldn't be much company as I'd be working," she said, putting emphasis on the last word.

"Right. All right then."

Not yet ready to let him and their past together go, she said as casually as she could muster, "Maybe we could go on the weekend. I'm off every Saturday and Sunday."

"Great. How about Saturday? What time?"

"Afternoon is good for me."

"Perfect. I'll pick you up."

Esther was on the phone with Maureen. She'd called her to tell her how the coffee date had gone with Derrick. As she filled in her cousin, she slid her fingers between the venetian blinds on her front window to take a peek outside. Her eyes widened in surprise when she spotted her mother, decked out as usual in bright colors, marching up her driveway. Today it was shades of red, orange, and yellow, and she wore a matching scarf on her head and oversized red glasses.

Esther interrupted her cousin. "I gotta go. My mother is here!"

"Did you know she was coming over?"

"No!"

"Okay. Call me right back after she leaves."

Everyone in their family knew that if Gail Campbell had to get something off her chest, especially when it came to her two daughters, she had a habit of showing up unannounced to voice her concerns and speak her piece.

"Knock, knock!" Gail called out before she stepped forward into Esther's home. Pebbles jumped up from her bed and ran to her, tail wagging, paws scrabbling over the floors.

"Hey, Mom. Where's Rufus?" Esther asked. Gail rarely went anywhere without her dog.

"DeeDee's walking him. Well, I use that verb loosely," Gail explained. "Anyway, he's out getting some fresh air."

"To what do I owe the pleasure?" Esther asked, deciding to do away with the pleasantries. She'd only just spoken to her mother the previous evening.

Gail pulled out a chair from Esther's kitchen table and sat down. "I'm here for a reason."

Esther said nothing and waited.

"I'll get to the point."

"Thanks, Mom, I appreciate that," Esther said smartly.

"I'm very unhappy that you and Suzanne are not speaking to one another," Gail said, her expression pained. "There is so much tension between the two of you."

Esther shrugged. "I don't know what to tell you."

Gail rolled her eyes. "Have you texted or called her?"

Esther certainly didn't want to cause her mother heartache, but she stood her ground and shook her head. "Nope." She added, "It is what it is."

"Don't give me that hooey. You know how I feel about family members not speaking." Gail spoke with firmness in her voice.

"I know, Mom."

"You know, but here we are."

"It will blow over," Esther said weakly.

"Will it? This is how this stuff starts out. You think it's all right because it's only been a few weeks, but let me tell you, those weeks will turn into months and then years until you won't remember what you stopped talking to one another about."

"That won't happen," Esther protested.

"Won't it? Wake up, it's happening. Do you want to miss out on her children growing up?"

"Of course not," Esther snapped. She cooled down and asked, "Didn't you and Aunt Louise ever have a serious argument? Ever?" Although Gail and Louise were very close, there had to have been some disagreements, especially when they were younger.

"As old as we are, we only fell out once. Stopped speaking to one another. We were young and stupid. And it was over a man. But things happened one night to make us see that we would never fall out again and certainly never over a man!"

Esther didn't know what to say to this. She was curious about what had happened and someday, she would ask either her mother or her aunt for the story.

Gail tilted her head to one side. "And did you think you could keep Derrick Radich a secret? Did you think no one would stop in my shop and tell me they'd seen you around town?"

"We were just catching up."

"At Java Joe's?"

Esther pressed her lips together.

"Is it serious?"

Esther scowled. "Of course not. He'll be going back to Florida soon."

"Let's hope so. We don't need you going through all that again. Anyway, getting back to my reason for stopping. I thought you and your sister were smarter than this," Gail continued.

"I don't like Ray. I don't like how he treats Suzanne. It's as simple as that," Esther said coolly.

"As far as Ray goes, sometimes I don't envy him."

Esther frowned. "Why?"

"It must have been very hard marrying into this family. The three of us were always very close, especially after your father died."

"It's not like I shun Ray or anything," Esther said, feeling it was a weak statement.

"No, but you haven't exactly rolled out the red carpet for him either."

Esther was about to grumble something but couldn't come up with anything.

Gail thumped a finger against the tabletop. "I'm asking you to fix this. Because I'm not going to stand for this not-talking-to-one-another business. You both know how I feel about these things. And your father wouldn't approve at all."

Esther's late father was always Gail's trump card. When she really needed to emphasize a point, she trotted him out for backup.

"Are you going to give this little pep talk to Suzanne?" Esther asked, realizing how petulant she sounded.

Gail stood from the table. "I'm on my way over there next."

In the past, Esther would have texted Suzanne to give her the heads-up, but today wasn't that day.

Chapter Nine

Cousin Rose arrived late Friday afternoon with her mother, Lydia, and her two kids, Becky and Connor. Once Esther was finished with work, she went over to her mother's house to see them. She inquired as to Suzanne's whereabouts and her mother said, "She'll be over in the morning."

"Esther!" Rose said and swept her up in a big hug. Esther recognized the familiar scent of Anthropology's Pearl perfume, a fragrance that was currently almost impossible to obtain.

Esther grinned. "Rose, it's great to see you."

"It's been too long!"

She eyed her cousin. Close to Esther in age, she was still stunning. She'd gotten her height from her father—if Esther remembered correctly, Rose stood at five eleven. She had the long legs of the Campbells, something neither Esther nor Suzanne had inherited. But her features and coloring, she'd inherited from her mother, who was of Norwegian heritage. Her hair was dark blonde, and everything about her face was perfect, from the blue eyes to the high cheekbones and the straight white teeth. You'd almost be jealous of Rose because her looks were truly breathtaking, but she was so nice and so much fun, you couldn't hold it against her. If her looks were a concept, she'd be sunshine and warmth.

Esther turned to her aunt and hugged her. Lydia's hug was gentler. "Aunt Lydia, you look great!"

Her aunt must be pushing eighty, but she appeared in good health. Although she shared Rose's looks, she did not share her height. Esther concluded that her aunt must have been a looker in her youth.

On the other side of Lydia were Rose's kids.

"Becky and Connor," Esther said. "You've gotten taller since the last time I saw you."

Becky smiled politely and Connor stared at her, unsure. They'd warm up soon.

"Come on, sit down, I've got snacks," Gail said.

Rose led the way to the table, taking a seat. She was flanked on either side by her children, and her mother sat across from her.

Esther helped Gail carry snacks over to the table. There was rye bread dip, spinach dip with Triscuits, and fruit salad with a cream cheese dip.

Gail stood, hands on the back of a chair, and asked the children, "What would you like to drink? I've got Pepsi, iced tea, lemonade, and water. Or milk." To the last one, Connor scrunched up his nose.

Gail laughed and said, "That's what I thought." She turned to her sister-in-law. "Lydia?"

"Lemonade is fine."

"Lemonade is fine for me too," Rose said. She turned to the kids. "What would you like to drink?"

In unison, they said, "Pepsi."

Esther helped her mother carry glasses over to the table, and they passed around the beverages.

"How was your flight?" Esther asked.

"It was fine," Rose replied. "Glad to be here."

"What made you come up to Lavender Bay?" Aunt Gail said.

"I always talk about Lavender Bay to the kids, how it was a great place to grow up, living so close to the beach, and how quaint the town is. I thought, I really should show it to them before they grow up. And we were long overdue for a visit."

"When was the last time you were home?" Esther asked.

"The last time was when I was pregnant with Becky. Fifteen, sixteen years ago?" Even scrunching up her face to think, Rose was still beautiful. There was no look that looked bad on her.

"Well, it's good to have you here," Gail said.

"There's so much to do here," Esther said. "There's the beach. And now they've got food trucks in the beach parking lot."

"I heard," Rose crowed. "And I'm anxious to try those grilled PBJs at Angie's food truck."

"What are your plans?" Esther asked.

"They've been invited to Suzanne's for a barbecue tomorrow afternoon," Gail told her.

"That's great." It smarted that Esther hadn't been invited, but she reminded herself she'd be at the beach with Derrick.

"And they're joining us at Louise's on Sunday morning for coffee," Gail said.

"Great!"

"And I've heard about Louise's coffee mornings! What a great idea," Rose said enthusiastically. "I wish we had more family down in Florida." She looked at Lydia. "Mom's family is pretty spread out across the country."

"I'm off on Sundays," Esther said. "If you'd like, you're welcome to come over Sunday afternoon to go swimming."

"That sounds nice. I've heard all about your pool," Lydia said. She looked fondly at her grandchildren. "Both Becky and Connor are great swimmers."

Esther tried to engage the two kids in conversation but was met with one- and two-word answers. She figured it was down to fatigue and left them alone. At ten o'clock,

Lydia stood up and said, "I hope you don't mind if I go upstairs and go to bed. I'm beat."

"Of course not. You know where everything is?" Gail asked.

"I do, and thank you for your hospitality, Gail. You're a good egg," Lydia said. She turned toward her grandchildren. "Would you like to go upstairs?"

They nodded and stood, chairs scraping. Everyone said goodnight and Rose said, "You don't mind if I stay down here for a bit? I'm not quite ready for bed."

"Not at all," Gail said.

She looked satisfied and helped herself to some rye bread dip. There was the sound of footfall upstairs as Lydia and the kids got ready for bed.

"Your kids are so grown up," Esther said. She went over to the fridge. "Rose, would you like a glass of wine?"

"Please."

"Red or white?"

"Doesn't matter. Whatever you bring over, I'll drink it."

"Mom, what about you? What would you like?"

"There's a bottle of Pinot Noir, why don't you bring that over," Gail said.

"Got it." She opened a bottle and let it breathe while she gathered wine glasses and carried them over to the table.

"Your children are lovely, Rose," Gail said.

"They are good kids," Rose said softly. "I'm lucky."

"Still no contact with their father?"

There was a flash of anger behind Rose's eyes. "No. As soon as he married his second wife, he moved to California and the kids never heard from him again."

"That's awful," Gail said with a shake of her head.

Esther sighed in sympathy. She could never quite grasp the idea of some parents not taking an interest in their young children.

"Hey, I'm perfectly all right with not seeing him for the rest of my life, because he was a real tool," Rose said, but then her tone softened. "But how do you explain to your children that their father wants nothing to do with them?"

"That's a tough one," Gail said.

"At least they have you and your mom," Esther said. In the whole scheme of things, grandparents were important. She thought of her own: Mark and Diana Sturges. They'd been nothing short of awesome.

"They're struggling a little bit," Rose admitted. "Each in their own way."

"Then it's up to us to make sure they have a great time while they're here," Esther said.

Gail lifted her glass and clinked it against the other two. "I agree. Cheers."

Chapter Ten

No one was sorrier than Esther that she'd agreed to go to the beach with Derrick. After an hour, there was sand everywhere. It stuck to the perspiration that covered her body, and it had even found its way into her teeth. She couldn't manage to get rid of that gritty feeling in her mouth. She wanted to go home and rinse her mouth out with a bucket of water.

Beside her, Derrick was stretched out on his beach chair, legs in the sand. She was glad he'd thought to bring something for them to sit on. She didn't want to think about where all the sand would be if she were on her back on a blanket. Likely in places she didn't even know she had. She wondered if it was too soon to go home.

Overhead, the sun blazed in the clear blue sky.

"Boy, that sun sure is hot," Derrick said.

"It is," Esther said, frowning. She'd forgotten to bring her hat, and her scalp was baking. The combination of the frown with the sweating was not a good look on her. So much for trying to impress an old flame.

"I love the beach," Derrick said with a sigh.

"That's good."

He looked over at her, seated next to him. "That's one thing I miss about Lavender Bay, you know, the beach."

"Aren't there beaches in Florida?" she asked smartly.

Chuckling, he said, "Of course. But I prefer freshwater lakes." He stood. "I'm going in the water. Do you want to go for a swim?"

"Sure," she said. Not ideal, but at least it would rinse off the sand that clung to her body. There was nothing to be done for her mouth. She couldn't actually rinse and spit from her water bottle. How would that look?

They walked into the water together, and although the lake was as warm as bathwater, it was refreshing. At the shore the water was clear, but the bottom was lined with rocks and pebbles. Groups of tiny minnows flittered over the rocks and dispersed as Esther and Derrick waded through. Esther walked gingerly, only wincing once or twice as she stepped on a rock the wrong way. Her pool at home came to mind with its smooth bottom and clear water.

They strode out farther until the water was up to their midsections. Esther's body began to cool down, but the lake was murky here; she wished she could see what was going on beneath the surface. She sighed. Derrick went out a little farther and dived in. She wouldn't be doing that. It wasn't like she'd be able to open her eyes underwater. You wouldn't be able to see anything anyway.

Her foot touched something unidentifiable, and she jumped. She splashed water over her shoulders to cool down. Derrick swam off, making smooth strokes with his arms. She watched him, mesmerized. He was a great swimmer. His movements were fluid and he glided through the water. After a while, when it seemed he might swim off to Canada, she began to make her way back to shore, trying not to think of all the things she couldn't see from her waist to her feet.

The beach was packed. In both directions were groups of people, brightly colored beach umbrellas, chairs, and blankets. The smell of coconut suntan lotion hovered in the air.

Back on dry land, she strode across the beach to their chairs. By the time she reached them, her wet feet and ankles were covered with thick clumps of sand. Within a few minutes, Derrick joined her. He was out of breath, and he pulled his towel off the chair and dried off his chest and shoulders. Esther turned her head away, thinking it felt voyeuristic to stare. He collapsed in a heap next to her.

"How about dinner tonight?" he asked. "The lawyer for Dad's estate recommended a great seafood place about ten miles up the highway."

Esther scrunched up her nose. "I really don't like seafood."

Derrick found this funny. "Still? You live next door to a lake. How can you not like seafood?"

She smiled, noting the irony of it. "I know. I prefer red meat."

"That's not good for your arteries or your digestive system."

Esther shrugged. "I suppose not, but a medium-rare steak is hard to beat."

"Sea bass could beat it."

"Is that the one where they serve it with the eye looking at you?"

He burst out laughing.

"I wouldn't be able to eat something while the thing was watching me do it." She shook her head. It took all kinds, she guessed.

Despite her dislike of the beach, she was enjoying Derrick's company. He was easy to talk to and pretty relaxed. In the end, she agreed to go out to dinner with him as long as the restaurant served both seafood and steak. Laughing, he agreed.

The following morning, Esther made her way over to her aunt's house for Sunday coffee. Although her sister sometimes missed these gatherings, Esther was a regular.

Family was too important to her to not be there. And that included extended family.

She was running late because one of the cats, Billy Bojangles, had decided it was time to check out a potted plant that had been there for years, thus knocking it over, and she didn't want to have to deal with potting soil all over her carpet when she returned later. From his perch on the cat tree, he watched her with disinterest as she cleaned up after him.

When she walked through the front door of Aunt Louise's house, she realized that everything was in full swing. There was raucous laughter coming from the kitchen, and she immediately recognized the voices of her mother and her aunt. She shook her head, laughing. Those two were always up to no good.

"There she is!" Aunt Louise called out when she appeared in the doorway.

"We were starting to get worried about you!" Gail chimed in. "I was about to send over a search party."

"Ha-ha. Billy made a mess and I had to clean it up," Esther said with a sigh.

"Is Billy your boyfriend?" Aunt Lydia asked.

Esther laughed. "No, worse. He's my cat."

Now everyone at the table was laughing. Mostly everyone was there except Angie and Tom, who were away for the weekend, and Suzanne and her family. But Nadine and Maureen and their families were present as were

DeeDee and her boyfriend, Brett Jovanovic, Lavender Bay's veterinarian.

Esther took the vacant seat next to Rose. Connor sat on the other side of his mother, taking everything in. Across the table, Becky sat next to her grandmother. Both children were very quiet. Esther felt sorry for them. The Cooks and the Campbells were a loud and boisterous lot and not for the faint of heart. They must be overwhelming to people who weren't used to them.

"How'd it go over at Suzanne's?" Esther asked her cousin.

Rose nodded, helping herself to a donut from the box in the center of the table. "We had a great time. Ray's a master chef with a grill."

"That's good," Esther said. No sense in badmouthing Ray in front of her cousin. That wouldn't be nice. Best to let Rose form her own opinion.

"Actually, they invited us to go to the beach with them today, but I told Suzanne we were going to your house to swim."

"That's all right. I'll send Suzanne a text and invite them over as well," Esther said, thinking Becky and Connor might want to hang out with people their own age. Sophie was Becky's age and Connor was close in age to Patrick.

At the other end of the table, Gail and Louise leaned into each other, whispering, and burst out laughing.

Rose smiled toward them. "Those two are a hoot."

"Oh, they're a hoot all right," Nadine piped in.

"They were like that forty years ago," Lydia said. "It always made me wish I had a sister."

Esther didn't say that she sometimes wished she was an only child, or at the very least had a sister who could see some sense.

Rose and her family enjoyed coffee morning, and then they all trekked over to Esther's house for the afternoon. On her way out the door, Esther told everyone it was an open invite. She texted her sister inviting her, Ray, and the kids. Suzanne never replied, but she did drop off her four kids later to go swimming. Although Esther was unimpressed with Suzanne for not coming in to say hello, she was happy to see her nieces and nephews. As she, Rose, Gail, and Aunt Lydia sat around the pool, enjoying the sunshine, Esther kept an eye on her nieces, nephews, and Rose's children. Connor fit in easily with Patrick and Jason, and soon the three of them were playing Marco Polo in the pool. Becky sat on the diving board, watching all the action, looking bored. Sitting at the bar behind them, Sophie and Margret stared at their phones and nursed Pepsis.

Esther decided to take things into her own hands. On one of her trips back into the house, she paused at the bar where her nieces sat. "Why don't you ask Becky to join you? She's out there sitting all by herself."

Sophie rolled her eyes.

"Come on, Soph," Esther said, smiling. "Don't be like that. You must know how it feels to be somewhere where you know no one."

Both girls shrugged, looking uninterested.

"Is Julia still going out with Jamie?"

"Yes," Sophie said sharply.

"Here's an opportunity for you to have a friend to do something with. She's only here for two weeks."

"I suppose."

"Didn't you see the sign on the way in?"

"What sign, Aunt Esther?" Margret asked, smiling, her mouth full of dental metal.

"No moping allowed. It's summer!"

This resulted in giggles from Margret and the hint of a smile from Sophie.

When neither niece said anything, Esther said, "I'm not asking you to become besties with her. But do me a solid and be kind to our guest, who happens to be your second cousin."

"All right, Aunt Esther, we'll see what we can do," Sophie said. "Come on, Margret."

Both girls slid off the bar stools and headed in the direction of the diving board where Becky sat.

Esther watched them, thinking, *That's that then.*

Late afternoon, after they'd consumed a couple of pizzas Esther had ordered and had delivered, Sophie suggested all the kids go for a walk through the town to show Becky and Connor around.

Esther was all for it. "That's a great idea."

The girls donned coverups over their swimsuits, and the boys trekked behind them with their swim trunks and shirts on, all clad in flip-flops. As Esther herded all six kids through the house to the front door, she slipped Sophie a few bills. "If you want to get ice cream later, here's some money for Scoopalicious."

"Thanks, Aunt Esther." Sophie smiled. She looked at her sister and Becky. "Come on, ice cream's on Aunt Esther."

"Remember to be back by the time the streetlights are on," Esther reminded them.

They all nodded. Esther closed the door behind them and headed back through the house toward the backyard. She ran into Rose, who was carrying the leftover pizza boxes inside.

"Where do you want me to put these?" Rose asked.

"You can leave them. I can get all that later."

"Nonsense. You've given us a great afternoon," Rose said, "and I appreciate it."

Esther relieved her of the pizza boxes. One still held three-quarters of a pizza. "Why don't you take that box home with you later? The kids might want that. I wouldn't eat it all myself."

"Thanks, Esther."

"Be right back." Esther carried the empty boxes out to the garage, where she threw them in the garbage bin wheelie. They were too greasy to recycle.

When she returned to the kitchen, Rose was standing there waiting for her, leaning against the sink. Esther wanted to shake her head. Her cousin even made that look good. Like she was doing a photoshoot.

"Thanks for encouraging the girls to talk to Becky," Rose said.

"No problem. Sometimes these kids need a little push."

"Or a smack," Rose said bitterly.

"What do you mean?"

Esther pulled the pitchers of lemonade and iced tea out of the refrigerator to bring outside.

Rose rested her hands behind her on the edge of the countertop. "One of the reasons I wanted to come up here was for Becky to have a change of scenery."

"Is she struggling a bit?" Esther asked. *The poor girl.*

Rose blew out a sigh. "She's been the victim of a terrible bullying campaign by a group of girls at her school. It started last year."

"Oh no," Esther said, feeling her heart drop. A queasy feeling formed in her stomach. With hormones and changes and trying to navigate your way to adulthood, the teenage years were difficult enough without being picked on. Esther sat down at the kitchen table and waved her cousin over to join her. Maybe she didn't have children, but she was certainly happy to lend a sympathetic ear.

Rose settled in the seat next to her and continued her story. "It started last year in the eighth grade. For whatever reason, a group of girls at the school decided that they needed to bully Becky."

"Have you talked to the school?" Esther asked. That seemed like the first stop.

Rose nodded. "Went to the principal, spoke to the teachers, and there was even a meeting with the other girls' parents."

"And it still continued?" Esther couldn't hide her surprise.

"If anything, it got worse."

"Seriously?"

"Yes. So, I transferred her to a different school."

"And did things improve?"

"Initially, yes," Rose said. "But one of the girls there knew someone from Becky's old school, and the bullying started all over again."

"That's awful." Kids could be so cruel.

"The problem is, they're very sly about it. They say nothing to her face. They don't even acknowledge her, but they've started a social media campaign against her and when the posts come to the attention of the school, they're suddenly deleted."

"How awful," Esther repeated. When she was growing up there'd been no social media and looking back, she thought they'd been better off. "And how is Becky coping?"

"Initially, she just ignored them, but it's gone on for so long they've managed to wear her down."

"What about her friends?"

"She had a few friends, but then they began to be targeted by these girls, so they distanced themselves from Becky."

Bullied and isolated. There was a part of Esther that wanted to cry out and protest at the cruelty of other people and the harshness of life.

"Her personality has changed. She's gone quiet and depressed. She's seeing a therapist, but I don't know if it's helping."

Esther didn't know what to say. "I'm glad you came up here then. We'll keep her busy and make sure she has a good time."

Rose's eyes filled with tears. "You know, you guys are really great."

Esther smiled. "I don't know about that. But I'm glad you told me this. I'll help any way I can."

"Your mom has been wonderful to us. It's not easy living alone and having four people show up on your doorstep."

"Yes, Mom does have her moments," Esther concurred.

"By the way, Connor loved coffee morning. He couldn't believe that you get to eat donuts and pastries every Sunday morning. I think you've got a convert."

"Great! The more the merrier."

The sliding glass door opened, and Gail poked her head in. "What are you doing in here? It's beautiful outside."

"We're on our way. We were having a chat."

"Well, bring it out here," Gail said. "And bring the iced tea and lemonade out. Lydia and I are parched."

"On it, Mom," Esther said. With a chuckle, she added, "Like I said, she has her moments."

As they walked outside, Esther told her cousin, "Look, Rose, if you need anything or if I can do anything, please let me know."

"I will, Esther."

Chapter Eleven

Esther carried her coffee over to an empty table. She noted Edna Knickerbocker and Edith Bermingham present in the café, at separate tables, but with their backs to one another. Esther didn't know how that had happened—the staff here at Coffee Girl must be slipping. They usually did their best to keep the sisters as far apart as possible. Currently, each sister attended to her own coffee and pastry without looking at or acknowledging the other. If you didn't know them, you'd never suspect they even knew each other, let alone that they were sisters. They looked like a pair of total strangers.

Suzanne walked in, and Esther was surprised to see her. She hadn't seen her or heard from her in a couple of weeks. To be fair, Esther hadn't contacted her either. Her sister walked up to the counter, placed her order, and turned around, looking for a table. She chose one at the far side of the café. Whether she'd seen her or not, Esther didn't know.

This is ridiculous, she thought. Two pairs of sisters sitting at four tables. She finished the rest of her pastry, picked up her coffee, and headed to Suzanne's table.

Suzanne looked up and her posture stiffened.

"Can I join you?" Esther asked.

"Sure."

Esther pulled out the chair and sat down. "How are things?"

"Good."

"You're still mad at me?"

"And you're still mad at me," Suzanne shot back.

Esther was about to say something when they were approached by Mrs. B.

Mrs. B smelled of her signature perfume, Chanel No 5. Her white hair was coiffed from her weekly trip to her hairdresser, and her face was lightly powdered.

"Hello, Esther, hello, Suzanne," Mrs. B said with a gentle nod of her head. "I heard a rumor that your cousin, Rose, is home for a visit."

"That's right," Esther said.

"The beauty queen of Lavender Bay," Mrs. B said with a fond smile.

Esther and Suzanne smiled.

Mrs. B continued, "Rose Campbell had the looks of a film star. She reminded me of myself when I was younger. Of course, I wasn't as beautiful as she was, but I did manage to find three husbands, so I was no slouch."

"More like you went through three husbands. And don't forget you discarded two of them," said Mrs. Knickerbocker. She'd joined the group but stood on the other side of the table, clear of her sister. Esther and Suzanne exchanged a look.

"You shouldn't comment on what you know nothing about," Mrs. B said coolly.

"I know plenty, Edith," Mrs. Knickerbocker snapped.

"You always were a know-it-all," Mrs. B retorted.

Esther cut in before things escalated. "Mrs. B, will I tell Rose to drop in on you before she goes home to Florida?"

The interruption diminished the rising tension. Both elderly women turned their attention to Esther.

"Yes, I would appreciate that," Mrs. B said. To Esther and Suzanne, she said, "Good day."

Edna lingered after her sister departed, which prompted Suzanne to ask, "Would you like to join us, Mrs. Knickerbocker?"

Edna shook her head. "No thank you, dear, I just wanted to put some distance between my sister and me. I'm on my way to Gloria's gift shop. Time to get another gag gift for Hal. Ta-ta!" And she was off.

Once both sisters were gone, Suzanne sipped her coffee and picked absentmindedly at her half-eaten cinnamon bun. "I heard a rumor that you've been keeping company with Derrick Radich."

Esther tried to appear as nonchalant as she could. "And?"

"I heard that you were spotted in Java Joe's looking all cozy, and then you spent a day at the beach with him. You hate the beach!"

"He's in town, we ran into each other, and we went for coffee."

"Derrick Radich?" Suzanne's tone indicated disapproval.

Esther's laugh was brittle. "We're only catching up, that's all."

"I hope so, after what he did to you," Suzanne said.

"It was a long time ago," Esther said. "I've moved on."

"Good for you. But I remember Christmas being ruined as Mom and I were left to pick up the pieces."

What was this all about? When had Suzanne become so aggressive?

"I'm sorry you were so inconvenienced," Esther said angrily. She gulped down the rest of her coffee.

"You know, Esther, I don't understand you. You had a good thing going with Lou, and you threw that aside. And now you're 'catching up' with Derrick Radich, of all people?" Suzanne's use of air quotes made Esther see stars.

"I don't know why this is any of your business," Esther said sharply.

Suzanne scowled. "You can comment on my life and my marriage, but your personal life is off-limits? Well, get ready, because I'm going to be sticking my nose in and letting you know just how I think you should live your life. Welcome to the club."

Esther wanted to clap back but decided it wasn't worth it. She stood up.

"Leaving so soon?" Suzanne said.

"Yes. I can't sit here all day. I've got things to do."

"Unlike those of us who don't have anything to do," Suzanne said smartly.

"Whatever," Esther said, picking her phone up off the table. "Goodbye, Suzanne."

Suzanne rolled her eyes. "Goodbye, Esther."

Chapter Twelve

Esther was wrapping up an IT help session with a client when she heard her side door open. Pebbles made a run for the door, tail wagging. There was a halfhearted bark followed by the sound of her jumping around. Soon Jason, Suzanne's youngest child, appeared. Esther loved all of her sister's kids, but this little boy had stolen her heart. Born eight weeks premature, he'd given everyone a fright in the beginning, but he'd survived and thrived.

She clamped her lips together when she got a full view of her nephew. He wore his swimming trunks, a pair of flip-flops, and a pair of goggles hanging around his neck, which she assumed to be new as she'd never seen them before.

"Did you want to go swimming?" she guessed.

"Yeah."

Esther glanced at her screen, saw there were no further calls, and stood from her desk, disconnecting from her headset. "What's wrong, buddy?"

He flung himself on her couch, swinging his legs. "Mom's in a bad mood."

"Why?" Esther asked. What had Ray done now? If she were married to Suzanne's husband, she'd be in a bad mood all the time.

He shrugged his little shoulders. "I don't know. She said she wished she were an only child."

With that, Esther burst out laughing. "I do too!" The little boy smiled.

Esther signed off and went and changed into her swimsuit. When she returned, Pebbles was curled up on the couch next to Jason.

"Does your mother know you're here?" she asked.

He shook his head. "I told her I was going out to play."

Suzanne would be frantic. "Before we jump into the pool, you've got to call your mother and let her know where you are."

"Do I have to?"

"Yes. You don't want her to be worried."

She handed him her cell phone, and he swiped through her contact list and put the phone to his ear.

"Hi, Mom, it's me, Jason." He petted the top of Pebbles's head as he listened. "I'm at Aunt Esther's. I'm going swimming. Chillax." He briefly held the phone away from his ear. "Do I have to? Yeah, okay." The smile was gone from his face.

He set Esther's phone on the coffee table.

"What did she say?" Esther asked.

"She was grumpy," he muttered. "She said I have to be home by five thirty for dinner because I have baseball practice tonight."

"Then we better get into the pool," Esther said. She pulled open the sliding glass door and followed Jason outside.

"Life vest, please," she said.

"Aw, do I have to?"

"You know the rules."

Once his life jacket was on, he jumped into the deep end of the pool. Keeping one eye on him, she went to the outdoor cabinet and grabbed a towel for herself.

"Did you see that, Aunt Esther?" he said as he came up from below the surface.

"I sure did. Which towel did you want? Spiderman or Batman?"

"Spiderman."

"Spiderman it is then," she said.

She laid the towels on the chair and stepped into the pool, sitting on the steps so that the water came up to her waist, keeping her eye on Jason.

The sliding glass door opened and Derrick appeared, and Esther's first feeling was one of annoyance. She hadn't known he was coming over. He never said. And did he always just walk into people's houses without knocking or ringing the doorbell? They'd gone for coffee again the other morning, but she didn't think they were at the stage where they could stop over at each other's homes unannounced. She told herself he was a guest and not to be cranky about it. *Gosh, Esther*, she thought, *you're like an old woman sometimes.*

"Hi there," she said.

"Hi there yourself," he said, closing the door behind him. "I was in the neighborhood and thought I'd drop in."

"No problem. We're having a swim."

Jason treaded water in the deep end, evaluating Derrick.

"Derrick, this is my nephew, Jason. Jason, this is an old friend of mine, Derrick."

"Mom said he's an old flame," Jason said.

"Well, that too," she said with a laugh.

"He's an honest little guy," Derrick said, taking a seat in one of the lounge chairs.

Esther stepped out of the pool and Derrick handed her a towel, watching her. She wrapped it around her waist. "Do you want a beer?"

He shook his head. "I'm driving."

"Lemonade or iced tea?"

"Either, whatever you grab first."

From the backyard refrigerator, she pulled out a pitcher of iced tea and poured two glasses. She also took out a juice box, figuring when Jason got out of the pool, he might want something to drink.

She handed Derrick his glass and set the juice box on the table between them. "What brings you here?"

"You, of course."

She smiled. He still knew how to say the right thing. There were moments when Derrick made her feel like that hopeful young girl she'd once been. The mature Esther chose not to examine that feeling too closely but simply to enjoy the moment.

"Hey, did you hear that Edith Bermingham is in the hospital?"

Esther shook her head. "No, I didn't hear that. Do you know why?"

"I heard she had a heart attack."

She couldn't help wondering how Mrs. Knickerbocker was taking this news. If she heard Suzanne was in the hospital, how would she feel? Not good, she concluded.

"Esther?"

"Huh?"

"I lost you there for a second," Derrick said.

She shook her head. "I'm sorry. Poor Mrs. B—I hope she's all right. What were you saying?" She cast a glance toward Jason, who was splashing around in the pool.

"I said I was surprised to come back to town and find Mrs. Knickerbocker and Mrs. B were still not on speaking terms."

"Unfortunately, yes. See? You come home to Lavender Bay and it's like you never left."

He smiled. "That's true. There's been a strong sense of déjà vu this trip, if you know what I mean."

"I think I do," she said quietly.

Jason climbed out of the pool from the deep end and yelled, "Aunt Esther, can I skim the pool?"

"Yeah, sure, go ahead."

He picked up the skimmer from the ground and walked around the pool, sliding it at an angle across the top of the water and then shaking the net free of any bugs, like Esther had taught him.

"I'm going to extend my stay here in Lavender Bay," Derrick said.

"Really?"

"Yes." He picked up his glass and drained it. "There's no rush to get home to Florida."

"What about work?" asked the sensible Esther.

"It'll survive another week or two without me."

"That's great," she said.

"I've really enjoyed spending time with you, Esther, and getting to know you all over again."

"Me too," she said.

They sat in the moment until a thought occurred to her. "Do you know what time it is?" she asked.

He picked up his phone, which he'd set on the table. "Five fifteen."

She looked over at Jason, who'd abandoned the net and was in the small shed, pulling out a float. "Hey, buddy, you better dry off. It's time to go home."

"Aw, do I have to?" he asked, holding the float by his side.

"Afraid so. Your mom said five thirty."

He mumbled to himself and threw the float back into the shed.

"I can drop him off at home if you want," Derrick offered. "But you'll have to tell me where Suzanne lives."

That would go over well, she thought. Him showing up at her sister's house to drop off Jason. Suzanne would probably have a cow.

"Thanks, but I'll do it, I've got some errands to run anyway," she said.

"Want some company?" he asked.

She was about to say yes, but hesitated. "No, that's okay. But thanks. How about lunch tomorrow?"

"Sounds good. Annacotty Room?"

She smiled. "You know me so well."

Jason made his way over, picked up the Spiderman towel, and gave his body a few swipes.

"Okay, I'm dry," he said seriously, water dripping from his swimsuit.

Esther laughed. This kid was too much. She and Derrick stood, and Derrick surprised her by leaning over and kissing her on the cheek. Her heart beat a little faster.

"Yuck," Jason said, scrunching up his face in disgust.

Esther and Derrick laughed.

They parted ways in the driveway, and Jason jumped into the back of Esther's car. She watched as Derrick drove away in his rental, a pickup truck. She was amazed that the feelings she'd had for him more than twenty years ago still existed on some level, albeit a small one.

Once Jason was buckled in, she drove over to her sister's house.

She pulled into the driveway and said, "Here you go, sir."

He leaned forward between the two front seats. "Can I come over swimming tomorrow?"

She nodded. "Sure. If your mom says it's all right."

She didn't bother going in, not knowing what kind of reception she'd get. But she watched and waited until Jason was up on the front porch. He turned and waved to her before disappearing into the house.

Chapter Thirteen

Esther pulled out a chair and sat at the kitchen table. The space was bright, with natural light streaming in through big windows. Suzanne sat across from her. The two of them had been summoned to their mother's house.

Gail bustled around her kitchen, making a pot of coffee and waiting for the kettle on the stove to whistle so she could make tea. Without a word, she set down a plate of pastry hearts in the center of the table, along with a small stack of dessert plates. Mugs and spoons and sugar and creamer were already laid out. Esther and Suzanne avoided looking at each other. Despite being in their forties, being called over by their mother felt like being called to the principal's office.

There was no small talk among them as Gail went about the industry of hospitality. Finally, she set the pots of tea and coffee on trivets on the table and slid into her seat. She poured herself a mug of coffee and plated a pastry heart. Neither Esther nor Suzanne took a beverage or a baked good.

"You might as well have something to eat and drink because I think we're going to be here for a long time," Gail said.

Both went to protest, but Gail held up her hand. "We're not leaving until we air our grievances and the two of you are speaking to one another."

Esther peeked at her phone.

"Put your phones away, ladies. I'll preface this meeting with the fact that I'm sure you both know by now that Edith Bermingham is in the hospital. She's had a heart attack. My biggest fear is that you'll let this disagreement between you get out of hand and you'll be estranged like Mrs. Knickerbocker and Mrs. B, which is really very sad when you think about it."

Gail let that sink in before returning to the topic at hand. "I'll start by saying how disappointed I am in both of you."

Suzanne folded her arms across her chest in the classic defensive position.

"Never did I ever think," Gail went on, "that my two daughters would stop speaking to one another. I'm flabbergasted. Your father wouldn't like this one bit."

Esther had to concede that point; her father had been all about family, and he wouldn't have stood for any of this.

"Do the two of you want to be Edna and Edith two-point-oh?"

Neither Esther nor Suzanne responded. Esther didn't think her mother was looking for input from either one of them. This was more of a stern lecture, where responses were not required.

"And this is all over a man. Or men." Gail shook her head in disbelief.

"I'll speak first," Suzanne said. Esther lifted an eyebrow. Her sister wasn't usually so assertive. "I think you're making a mistake with Derrick."

"And I think you've made a mistake with Ray!"

"My marriage is none of your business."

"And who I hang out with is none of yours."

Suzanne snorted. "How can you be so sure he won't dump you again?"

"He can't dump me again because we're not in a relationship. We're just hanging out while he's home in Lavender Bay. Then he's going back to Florida and back to his life, and I'm going back to mine."

Suzanne persisted. "I heard he's staying longer than he intended."

"So what? He's settling his father's estate. He can stay as long as he wants. He doesn't need your permission," Esther said sharply. "Or mine."

"I think you're making a mistake, and I don't want to see you get hurt again."

That gave Esther pause. "I appreciate your concern, but I'm an adult and I can handle my own life. And my own affairs."

Gail laid her hand on the table toward Suzanne. "She's right. Esther has to handle her own life. If this turns out to be a poor choice, then she'll have to live with the consequences. It's not for us to interfere."

Her tone indicated she, too, thought it was a poor choice.

"Can I be honest?" Esther asked her sister.

"Honest or blunt?" Suzanne said.

Esther looked at her blankly.

"Say your piece, Esther," her mother encouraged.

"I don't understand why you stay with Ray," Esther said. "He's so controlling."

Her sister's face reddened. "How dare you butt into my marriage."

"Are you happy?" Esther challenged. Now both she and her mother looked at Suzanne, waiting for a reply.

"I'm content."

Esther snorted. "Content?!"

"You never took the time to get to know Ray," Suzanne said. "You passed judgment and decided you didn't like him from day one. Now, I'm sorry you were disappointed in love, but don't take it out on me, my husband, or my marriage."

Esther's temper flared. "I'm not taking anything out on you. I genuinely don't like your husband."

"Easy," Gail warned in a low voice.

Tears filled Suzanne's eyes. "Do you know how hard it is to be married to a man your family doesn't approve of? I'm in the middle, and it's a position I resent being in."

"It's not that we don't like Ray," Gail started.

Suzanne snapped her head in her mother's direction. "But you *don't* like Ray, Mother." Saying "Mother" instead of "Mom" was akin to their mother using their first and middle names when they were younger and she was calling them out on something. "That's the truth of it. But he is my husband. And you know what's really sad? This family goes on and on about closeness and togetherness and the importance of family, but none of you have gone out of your way to make my husband feel welcome."

Gail went to say something, but Suzanne continued to speak. "And you can get off your high horse about it. Ray's family treats me like one of their own. They don't put Ray into a position of being pulled between his marriage and his family. They're not perfect either, but they are accepting. Actually, you could take a lesson or two from them."

Esther didn't know what to say to any of that. By the time she went to say something, her sister had picked up her thread. "You think I should get a divorce and move on with my life. You're so arrogant to think you know what's best for me. Ray is the father of my children. We have created a family. Is our marriage perfect? No. Is he? No. Am I? No. But we keep trying."

Esther opened her mouth to speak, not sure of what to say. But her sister cut her off.

"You've got your panties in a bunch because we're expressing our concern about Derrick after only a few days, but then you're critical of my husband. You can't have it both ways, Esther." Suzanne stood and slammed the chair into the table. Holding on to the back of the chair with both hands, she said, "Not once have you asked me how *I* feel about Ray. You've just assumed that because you don't like him, neither do I. But here's the answer: despite everything, despite all our difficulties, I still love him. He has wonderful qualities that I admire. But how would you even know that? You never bothered to get to know him." She turned on her heel and stormed out of the house, slamming the door behind her.

Esther and her mother stared at the door Suzanne had just exited through. Finally Gail made a *tsk-tsk* sound and said, "It's Edna and Edith all over again." And the sigh that followed was full of sadness.

PART TWO

EDNA

Chapter Fourteen

The décor in Edna Knickerbocker's living room hadn't changed in the forty years since she'd bought the house: Hardwood floors covered with a large oval braided rug. Furniture best described as 1970s colonial, with heavy wood frames and cushions in a busy pattern of rust, brown, and cream. A wagon wheel coffee table she'd always found interesting. When her landline started ringing one afternoon from its perch on the end table, reverberating through the house, it startled the octogenarian. It was so rarely used that she could only wonder who could be calling. Probably one of those spam calls. Anyone she spoke to regularly knew she preferred her mobile phone and relied on that. It had those extra-large buttons, which helped with her failing eyesight.

She picked up the handset from the cradle, ready to hang up if the caller sounded fishy. "Hello?"

"May I speak with Edna Knickerbocker?" asked a female voice.

"This is she."

"My name is Linda. I'm a nurse over at Lavender Bay Medical Center."

Edna's first terrible thought was that something had happened to her dear friend, Hal. She'd seen him earlier that morning, but she supposed anything could happen at any time. Wasn't she only just telling her doctor that the other day?

Linda continued. "I'm calling on behalf of Edith Bermingham."

Edna's immediate reply was "Why?"

"Aren't you her sister?"

"I am."

"She has you listed as her next of kin," the nurse explained.

Edna couldn't hide her surprise. "She does? Is she all right?"

"Mrs. Bermingham has had a heart attack and has been admitted to the hospital. We're continuing to monitor her. Currently, she's in stable condition."

"Oh," was all Edna could say. How was she supposed to react to this news? She hadn't had a civil conversation with her sister in almost seventy years.

The nurse was speaking, but Edna missed it.

"Did you want her room number?" Linda repeated.

After only a slight hesitation, Edna said, "Of course. Hold on. I'll need to get a pencil." Balancing the handset between her ear and shoulder, she opened the drawer of the end table and pulled out an old puzzle book and a pencil. One end of the pencil had bite marks, and the other end badly needed to be sharpened.

"Go ahead," Edna told the nurse.

The nurse rattled off the room number.

"Thank you for calling," Edna said politely before hanging up. She sank down on the sofa, staring at the number she'd scribbled on the first page of the puzzle book. What was she supposed to do with this information? Was she supposed to visit her sister in the hospital? Did Edith want that?

For the next few hours, Edna struggled with this. She said nothing to anyone, not even Hal, whom she shared everything with. Her neighbor, a kind and peaceful man, had always encouraged Edna to reconcile with her sister. But she'd resisted. It was simply one of those things.

It left her questioning Edith's decision to list her as her next of kin. Edith had plenty of friends, friends she was close to that could have been named on the paperwork. Even now, at their age, Edna's younger sister continued to confound her.

1957

Edna Knickerbocker sat on the steps of her front porch with her next-door neighbor, Charley Maloney. It was early evening, and they'd stopped at Wasserman's drugstore for a root beer float on the way home from an afternoon at the beach. Her skin was warm from the sun, and there was still sand clinging to her feet. But she was happy.

She and Charley had been friends since they were four years old. They went through school together, always in the same grade, and because of their last names, Knickerbocker and Maloney, their desks were never that far apart. Without a doubt, she would say he was her best friend. They shared a love of the beach, of baseball, and of their favorite television show, *Gunsmoke*, which they always watched together on the Knickerbockers' black-and-white television set as the Maloneys didn't have one. Edna's mother said it was because they had too many kids to afford one.

Charley looked around. "Gosh, Edna, it's even quieter than usual around here. Where is everyone?"

"Mom's at work and Dad is putting in overtime at the garage. Grace Gibson needed her car fixed pronto." Edna's mother worked at Block's Answering Service. She'd gotten Edna a job there too, after graduation, but

Edna had already decided she didn't want to stay there long term. She never wanted to answer a phone again for as long as she lived. "And Edith is out on a date with that Jerry Melvin."

"Is she still seeing him? I'm telling you, Edna, he's no good," Charley said, his face earnest. To some, with his bright red hair and freckles, he would be deemed unattractive. But not to Edna. "You've got to tell her."

Edna snorted. "Edith would never listen to me. It would be a waste of my breath talking to her."

He shook his head. "He's bad news."

Edna said no more. She liked that Charley looked out for them, but she didn't want him being too interested in her sister's love life.

"Man, it sure is peaceful around here," he said again. "I love it over here."

"And I love it at your house. Want to swap?" she said, elbowing him.

The Maloneys had lived next door to the Knickerbockers for as long as Edna could remember. There were eight children, a mix of boys and girls. Edna loved going over to the Maloneys'. The house was constantly full of noise, and there was always something going on. It was pure bedlam. And for the most part, despite the vast number of people crammed into the home, they all seemed to get along. There was harmless bickering, of course, but it always seemed forgotten the next day. It was so unlike her own home, where she fought endlessly with Edith. They were all floating on a high next door as Charley's oldest brother was getting married soon. He'd be the first one to leave the nest. Mrs. Maloney had said more than once it would give them some breathing room.

"Did you say something, Charley?" Edna asked, coming out of her deep thoughts.

"It was a perfect day, wasn't it?" he asked.

"Yes, it was," she agreed.

"The sun was hot but not unbearable, and the lake was the ideal temperature."

"Almost like bathwater," Edna added.

"Exactly. Then we had that root beer float at Wasserman's drugstore, and it was the perfect mix of root beer and ice cream."

They often pooled their money and split a float. Two straws. Anyone who didn't know them would think they were boyfriend and girlfriend.

And somewhere between the time she was eighteen and now, she'd started seeing Charley in that way too, as more than a friend. She didn't know when it had happened, but she'd come to the slow realization that she was in love with him. One day, that's how it was. It was not a crush, she'd told herself. She knew him inside out and their friendship was solid, but still she loved him. So far, he hadn't shown any sign of reciprocating, but ever since putting a name to her feelings, she'd been living and breathing in a constant state of hope and longing and waiting.

"And look around, Edna," he said as his gaze swung up and down the street. "Look at all the flowers and the rosebushes."

She did as he asked, agreeing that everything looked pretty in the summer. Better.

Charley's laugh came easy to him, as usual. "If I mentioned to one of the guys about the rosebushes, they'd run me out of town on a rail."

Now they were both laughing.

They sat there, so close together you couldn't slide a sheet of paper between them. Edna's skin was bronzed from a summer spent in the sunshine. But as was the case with many redheads, Charley's pale, freckled skin didn't tan, only burned, so he was as fair now as he was on the first day of summer. Sometimes, Edna had to remind him to get out of the sun.

"You know what I—" Charley started, but his voice broke off as she unbent her golden legs and stretched them out in front of her. His eyes slid down the length of them, landing on her skinny ankles. Edna was aware of a tingly sensation that floated over her body.

He tried again. "You know what I like about you, Edna?"

Edna leaned back, trying to adopt a provocative pose along the lines of Marilyn Monroe or Jayne Mansfield. Charley looked at her and frowned. "You all right? You don't look so good."

Immediately, she sat up, abandoning the idea of becoming a seductress. She smoothed the hem of her shorts. "I'm fine. Now, what were you saying?"

He blinked. "Oh, yeah, right. What I was trying to say is, one of the things I like about you is you're so easy to talk to. You're like one of the guys."

Edna's resulting smile was shaky. She didn't want to be like one of the guys. She opted for straightforward. "We've been friends for a long time, Charley—"

"Our whole lives!"

She nodded. It seemed that way. "But I can assure you, I'm not one of the guys."

"I know that. You'd never be able to play football."

Edna pressed her lips together in a grimace. "I'll remind you that I can swing a bat as good as any fella around here." The last part came out a bit sharper than she intended.

Charley sighed, leaned forward, and laid a freckled hand against his forehead. "Sometimes the words I'm trying to say don't come out the way I want them to. Somehow, they get changed in transit."

He looked so momentarily forlorn that Edna couldn't help but reach out and lay her hand on his back. "It's okay, Charley," she said softly, "you don't need to have the right words for me."

There was a moment of stillness that floated between them and lingered. Charley opened his mouth to say something, but that was as far as he got. His head turned away from Edna toward the approaching figure of her sister.

Edith's face broke into a generous smile when she spotted Charley. Edna's posture sagged as she let out an inaudible sigh. Next to her, Charley sat up a bit straighter and appeared to suck in his stomach. Edna frowned. Her gaze traveled to her sister, wondering what the appeal was.

Edith was dressed in a pale pink dress with a full skirt, a cinched waist, cap sleeves, and a boat neck. She had on a hint of pink lipstick, and there was a light dusting of powder over her face. In her dark hair she wore a pink headband. Begrudgingly, Edna admitted to herself that part of her sister's allure was her femininity, and the way Charley was looking at her, it was apparently Kryptonite for him. It seemed as if he'd all but forgotten about Edna.

Edith stopped on the path in front of them.

"Hello, Charley," she said.

"Hello, Edith." Charley stood and stepped off the porch until he was next to her. He was so much taller than Edith that she had to look up at him.

Edna didn't think they looked so good together, he with all that red hair and her sister decked out in pink.

"Edith, I've got to say something," Charley said.

"What's stopping you?" she asked. She looked up at him from underneath her eyelashes. Edna scowled; her sister's demureness was dubious at best. Charley should get a glimpse of her when she was shouting at Edna or throwing her hairbrush.

Anyone with any bit of pride would easily see what was going on here. It was obvious that Charley was enamored with Edith. Edna wasn't blind, but she'd already staked her claim, if only mentally, and she wasn't about to give him up to a squatter, who had no rights as far as she was concerned.

"Edith," Charley was saying, "you've got to get rid of Jerry Melvin. He's no good."

"Did you have someone else in mind?" she asked softly, her gaze searching his face.

Charley stuttered, "Well, actually—"

Edna bounced off the porch. "Charley, Edith is able to make her own decisions as to whom she steps out with."

Edith pivoted toward her sister, her full skirt swishing around her tanned legs, and stared her down before returning her attention to the boy next door. "Charley, I appreciate any insight you might have. We should have a conversation sometime about this."

Beneath his freckles, Charley went red. "I'd like that."

"Great, we'll talk soon." She swished past him, narrowed her eyes at her sister, and went into the house.

Edna stood there, invisible, as Charley stared into the space Edith had vacated.

Oh, Charley.

Chapter Fifteen

Edna stood in the kitchen at the stove, frying up some pork chops for dinner. It was her day off and as her mother was working the four-to-midnight shift at the answering service, Edna cooked the dinner. The two windows in the kitchen were open, but the frying pan and the pot of boiling potatoes only made the kitchen more humid. Her bangs were plastered to her forehead. The back door opened, and Edna prayed it wasn't Charley, because sometimes domesticity was sweaty.

"Hey, Edna," said Charley, stepping into the kitchen. "Something smells good."

"Hi, Charley." Unable to help herself, Edna smiled. She lifted a pork chop and, satisfied that it was browned, flipped it and added a sliced onion to the pan.

"You're going to make someone a fine wife someday," he said with a nod toward the stove.

Glowing, Edna thought, *That's the plan.* "Sit down, Charley. Would you like something to drink?"

"No thanks," he said, and remained standing.

"Is everyone all excited about the wedding? It won't be long now," she said. It was less than a month away, and she'd been dropping broad hints that he'd have more fun if he brought a date. He'd have someone to dance with. But he seemed to be dragging his feet about inviting her to be his guest.

"No one's feet are touching the ground over at my house." His hands were in his pockets, and he shifted nervously on his feet.

Edna chuckled. "Are you all right? You're acting strange."

His head snapped up. "Am I?"

She nodded, still smiling.

He brushed the back of his head with his hand. "Look, is Edith around?"

Edna's smile disappeared. "She's upstairs."

Charley shoved his hands into his pockets. "Would you mind calling her for me, Edna?" A flush crept up to his cheeks.

Edna wiped her hands on her apron and said, "Sure, Charley." She walked to the bottom of the staircase and called up several times, but Edith's record player was so loud she never heard her. Grumbling, Edna stomped up the stairs to her sister's room and knocked on the door. Strains of "Be-Bop-A-Lula" emanated from the room.

"Edith?"

The door opened so quickly that Edna jumped back, startled.

"What?" Edith demanded.

Edna scowled at her. "Charley is downstairs, he wants to talk to you."

Her sister's expression softened. "I'll be right down." She closed the door. The record player went mute and by the time Edna had reached the top of the landing, Edith was right behind her. She'd put on some pink lipstick.

The three of them stood in the kitchen and Charley said, "Edith, can I talk to you privately for a minute?"

Edna frowned. Now what did Charley need to talk to her sister about in private? In the past, they'd never kept secrets from each other.

Charley followed Edith into the parlor, leaving Edna in the kitchen. Once they were out of sight, she tiptoed over to the doorway to listen unobserved.

"Um, Edith, I wanted to ask you something," Charley started.

"Go ahead," she encouraged.

He cleared his throat. "I was wondering if you would go with me to my brother's wedding."

Edna sagged against the doorframe. *No, Charley. Not Edith. Please.*

Edith said nothing but then she didn't have a chance, because Charley kept talking. "I know it's kind of last minute, but I'd really like you to go with me. You don't have to, though. I don't want you to think you *have* to go, but I think we'd have a lot of fun together . . ." His voice trailed off.

"I'd love to go to the wedding with you, Charley," Edith said softly.

"You would? Gee, that's swell," he said. There was the lift of his voice and the stuttering stopped. Amazing how a simple yes could instill someone with so much confidence. "I promise, we'll have a great time."

"I'm sure we will."

"That's great then," he said. "I'll see you around."

"I'm right here, next door."

Charley laughed that easy laugh of his. The way he laughed when he and Edna were joking around.

Edna's eyes stung, and she blinked several times to force back the tears. She smelled something burning. The pork chops! For a moment she forgot about her pain and raced to the stove. Smoke rose from the pan, and all the pork chops were black on one side.

"Drat!" she said. Quickly, she moved the cast iron pan to another burner. She'd somehow have to salvage them. There was nothing else to do for dinner.

Charley came through the kitchen, hands in his pockets, whistling. He paused and sniffed the air.

"Something burning?"

"Only the dinner, Charley," she grumbled.

"Edna?"

"What?" she snapped, looking over her shoulder. She was trying to scrape the burnt part off one of the chops.

"Your advice was sound, I'm glad I took it," he said, oblivious to her sour mood.

She half turned, scowling. "What do you mean?"

"You told me I should take someone to the wedding. Like a date."

"Yes, I did," she said, her voice high and shrill. She wanted to scream *I meant for you to ask me!*

"I've asked Edith. She said yes."

"That's wonderful." She could not keep the sarcasm out of her voice. Charley didn't notice.

"I'll talk to you later, Edna." He walked out the back door before she could even say goodbye.

Her instinct was to throw the meat in the garbage and rush upstairs and tell Edith what she actually thought of her. Tell her that Charley was off-limits. She abandoned the burnt pork chops on the stove, deciding she'd figure dinner out later. She pulled out a drawer and rummaged through it, knowing there was a pack of cigarettes buried at the back of it. Her mother had smoked briefly in an effort to lose weight but had not pursued it, not liking it. Once her fingers found the forgotten pack, she pulled it out, tapped out a cigarette, lit it, and sat down at the kitchen table to have a good think.

After careful consideration, she decided it was best to say nothing. Knowing both Charley and Edith as well as she did, she figured it would run its course. Charley would see through Edith's facade and realize Edna was truly the one for him. And Edith, she'd soon get bored with Charley. By the number of *Vogue* magazines stacked up in her bedroom, Edna had concluded that her sister had social aspirations, and Charley was in the middle of a plumber's apprenticeship. No, Edith wouldn't want a plumber long term. Edna had to be patient and bide her time.

Charley continued to come over in the evenings and sit on the porch, but it was Edith he came to see. Edna sat in the parlor, pretending to watch television, but mostly listening to their inane conversation. The things her sister talked about! Charley must be bored out of his mind. But he continued to seek her out every time he popped over. It was as if he'd forgotten his friendship with Edna.

"Do you want to go to the beach Saturday afternoon?" she asked one evening as he waited for Edith to come downstairs.

He looked at her as if he'd never seen her before. "Huh?"

Amused, Edna smiled and said, "The beach? Saturday?"

He shook his head. "I can't. I'm working a side job in the morning, and then I'm taking Edith to the movies Saturday night."

"Oh, all right," Edna said, her voice weak. "Another time."

"Yeah, sure."

Edith appeared on the front porch, looking very feminine in a pale green dress and minimal make up. Charley looked at her and his face lit up. Something inside Edna lurched forward, then sank back and shriveled up. With a mixture of emotions, she watched as Charley walked off with her sister.

Slowly, she went back into the house. Her father sat in the parlor, reading *The Lavender Bay Chronicles*. Her mother was working the four-to-twelve shift. Today was Edna's last day off as she would be starting a string of five days.

She looked through to the kitchen, but everything was done. The dishes had been washed and put away, and the table and the counter had been wiped down. Edna stood there, debating what to do. She didn't want to sit around and think about Charley and Edith being out together and what they were doing. But she couldn't focus on anything else.

Edwin Knickerbocker lowered his newspaper and studied his oldest daughter for a moment. "So they've gone then?"

"Yes."

He set the paper down and sighed. "Edna, sit down for a minute."

She sat down in the middle of the sofa.

Her father leaned forward in his easy chair, elbows resting on his knees. "Honey, I know you're sweet on Charley."

Edna lifted an eyebrow. Had she been that obvious? If even her father had seen it then everyone in Lavender Bay must know how she felt about Charley Maloney. Except for Charley.

"Don't worry, it was your mother who told me."

She looked down at her hands in her lap.

"The advice I would give you is to be patient," he said.

"Patient?" she repeated. "About what?"

"About Edith and Charley." He pushed the newspaper away and half turned in his chair. "Charley will come to his senses and see that Edith isn't for him in the same way that Edith will come to her senses and see that Charley isn't right for her."

"Does Mother say the same thing?"

He nodded. "Yes. We both think they're wrong for one another. They only need to realize that themselves."

Edna bit her lip. The unspoken fear was that they wouldn't. That things would progress and she would be left behind. Alone. Her father's theory echoed her own plan to bide her time, waiting for them to lose interest in each other. But it wasn't happening fast enough to suit her.

"So be patient," Edwin said again. "It will all work out, you'll see. It always does."

Edna wanted to believe him, she really did, but she was riddled with worry.

He picked up the newspaper and disappeared behind it, signaling that the conversation was over.

Chapter Sixteen

It was a great relief for Edna when the Maloney wedding was over. Of course, she was forced to listen to a recounting of the whole affair during Sunday dinner the following day. It was pure torture.

Her mother commented, "Edna, you haven't eaten much."

All eyes were on Edna's plate, which remained untouched. The truth was, she didn't think the food would get past the big lump in her throat.

"You should have seen the food at the wedding!" Edith said. And she went off in a flurry of describing the appetizer, main course, and dessert in painstaking detail.

Edna wanted to cry. Was she to live vicariously through her sister as she went out with the love of Edna's life? She reminded herself that the wedding was now over and hopefully, things would go back to normal. She thought of all the things she missed about Charley: their conversations about baseball and current events, the root beer floats they shared up at the drugstore, the days they spent at the beach, and most of all Charley himself.

As Edith prattled on about who wore what and the variety of hats, Edna stood to start clearing the table. As she carried the stack of plates to the kitchen, she bumped into Charley, who'd come in through the back door.

"Hi, Edna," he said, smiling. He leaned past her and waved to everyone still sitting at the table, his gaze coming to rest on Edith, who blushed.

"Are you ready, Edith?" he asked.

Edith laid down her napkin, stood from the table, and pushed her chair in. "I'm sorry, Charley, I was so busy telling Mother and Dad all about the wedding that I lost track of time." She disappeared from the room and could be heard running up the staircase.

"Are you going somewhere?" their mother asked Charley, and glanced sideways at Edna.

"To the beach. It's a beautiful day for it," Charley replied.

The forks and knives balanced on top of the plates Edna was carrying clattered to the floor. Charley bent over to pick them up. "Let me help you, Edna."

Edna stood there, frozen. Charley laid the dirty silverware on the plates. "There. No harm done."

Edna wanted to cry but she forced out a thank-you, brushed past Charley, and headed to the kitchen. She set the dishes in the sink and started to run the water but when the sink was half full, she turned off the tap, abandoned the task, and walked out the back door. She kept walking, wanting to get as far away as possible from her home and from Charley and Edith.

She walked blindly, with no destination in mind, wounded that the wedding was over and that neither seemed bored or finished with the other. It was like she had this large open wound that refused to close and heal. She thought of going to see her Aunt Lenore but decided she wanted no company, preferring instead to brew in her own melancholy. The beach was the ideal place to do that, but the last thing she wanted was to be a witness to Charley and Edith frolicking in the water.

Eventually, she found herself at Wasserman's drugstore. For a Sunday afternoon, it was pretty empty. She sat at the counter on one of the red vinyl swivel stools.

Dougie, the soda jerk, approached her, dressed all in white from his short-sleeved shirt to his pants to his peaked cap. There was a pencil tucked behind his ear. "Where's your partner in crime, Edna?"

She liked Dougie. He was in his second year of college and worked part time at the drugstore while he went to school. He was always nice to them. She forced a smile and shrugged. "I don't know," she lied.

"The usual?"

"Yes, please."

She stared at the countertop as if it were the most fascinating thing she'd seen in years. Dougie slid the root beer float across the counter to her.

"Thanks, Dougie."

"Oops, almost forgot." He smiled, passing her a straw.

Over the radio, Johnny Mathis's new hit, "Chances Are," drifted out across the drugstore. When she'd heard the tune for the first time, she thought it was the perfect song for her and Charley. That song, coupled with the lone straw, caused her to heave in a great big breath. She clamped her lips around the straw and drank, even though tears pooled in her eyes.

"Edna, do you mind if I sit here?"

Grace Gibson had approached, and Edna hadn't even seen her.

Edna removed her mouth from the straw and said, "Go ahead, Grace."

Grace sat on the stool beside Edna and set her handbag down on the counter. As she pulled off her white gloves, she said, "I was home and thought I could go for a banana split." She laughed to herself. "So I thought I'd come down and have one."

Edna nodded. Grace was dressed in a skirt and blouse that probably cost an arm and a leg. She'd more or less taken over the running of the Gibson's Grape Jelly factory from her father, who now enjoyed semi-retirement. She'd cut her hair short and now wore it curled around her face and above her ears. She wore bright red lipstick, and a single strand of pearls circled her neck. Edna wondered if she ever dressed casually, like in the capris and simple, sleeveless blouses Edna herself tended to favor. She couldn't picture it.

"Hiya, Miss Gibson," Dougie said. "What can I get for you?"

"Dougie, you can call me Grace."

"Okay, Miss Gibson."

She shook her head. "How about a banana split?"

"Coming right up." Dougie turned away and busied himself making Grace's request.

"How are you doing, Edna?" Grace asked.

"I'm fine." Edna nodded, taking another gulp of her float. It tasted flat. Maybe because Charley wasn't there to share it with her. She wondered if he ever brought Edith here and shared a float with her. That thought pained her.

"I'm surprised you're not at the beach today," Grace said. "It's such a beautiful day."

And with that, Edna burst out crying.

Alarmed, Grace leaned into her and asked, "Oh my goodness, what is it? What's wrong?"

Edna shook her head. Mortified, she could not open her eyes, and hoped the place remained empty.

"What's happened? Tell me, maybe I can help," Grace said.

Finally, Edna opened her eyes, her gaze landing on her half-finished float, the ice cream now melting. "It's nothing," she said with a big sniffle.

"No one cries over nothing." Grace reached for her handbag and pulled out a handkerchief, handing it to Edna.

"Thanks." Edna took the perfectly pressed floral square and dabbed at her eyes, thinking it wasn't appropriate to blow her nose into someone else's hankie. She sniffed again.

Dougie set Grace's banana split in front of her. His whistling had stopped. He looked at Edna for a moment and turned away to do something else.

Unable to help herself, Edna poured forth her story. How she loved Charley more than anything, but he had chosen her sister.

Grace made sympathetic noises. Clutching the handkerchief, Edna held her hands clasped in front of her, resting them against her forehead. She didn't think it was possible to feel so terrible but here she was, unable to stop crying.

Grace reached over and gently patted her back. This kindness made Edna cry harder. "It's very painful to love someone more than they love you."

Edna nodded.

"You think you're going to die."

Edna nodded some more, unable to speak through her tears.

"You have all this love to give, and they don't want it. At least they don't want it in the way you want them to want it."

Edna looked over at Grace. "You sound like you have some experience in this department."

Grace tilted her head slightly and said, "A little bit."

"How did you survive?"

Grace sighed. "I focused on other things. Threw myself into my work, that sort of thing."

Edna couldn't see herself throwing herself into work at the answering service. Already she was dragging her feet going in there.

"If not work, do something to shift your focus," Grace advised. "Travel maybe. I used to go see my friend in Kansas."

"Thank you, Grace, your advice is sound," Edna said finally. Whether she would follow it or not remained to be seen.

The topic changed and they conversed about ordinary and mundane things, and even though Edna's burden of heaviness remained, she didn't feel as bad as she did when she first walked into the drugstore.

Grace pushed her half-eaten banana split aside and chuckled. "My eyes are always bigger than my stomach."

"Thank you, Grace," Edna said. She held up the crumpled, damp handkerchief. "I'll wash this and get it back to you."

"Not necessary. I've got a drawerful of them at home." Grace stood and patted Edna on her shoulder. "Take care of yourself, Edna."

"I will, thank you."

Grace walked over to the cash register and paid her bill.

Edna waited a few moments, debating whether to finish what was left of her soupy float, but decided against it. She picked up her change purse off the counter and went to pay the bill.

"You're all set, Edna," Dougie said from behind the counter. "Miss Gibson paid for your float."

Edna looked toward the door where Grace had exited, touched by the kindness.

"All right, thanks, Dougie."

"Take care of yourself, Edna."

"You too." She left feeling slightly better, and Grace's words and kindness had contributed to that.

Chapter Seventeen

A few weeks later, things fizzled out between Edith and Charley. Her father had been right. She said nothing about it to her sister, deciding it wasn't worth it to rile her up. They'd never been the type of sisters to share confidences. Edith was unusually quiet, her barbed tongue mute, and that led Edna to speculate that maybe it was Charley who'd called it off.

For the first time in a while, Edna felt pretty good, and she walked with a spring in her step. And yet she hardly saw Charley. She kept looking for him, but he was either working or out with the guys. Her plan was to ask him to go to the beach over the weekend. Summer was winding down, and there wouldn't be too many warm days left to go swimming.

She'd give him time. In the meantime, she made plans for all the things they could do for the rest of the summer and the fall. She was sure that Charley would eventually realize that Edna was the one for him.

Edna's parents were in the kitchen when she arrived home from working the midnight-to-eight shift, otherwise known as the graveyard shift, at the answering service. Her eyes burned, and all she could think about was her bed upstairs.

"Morning," she said as she pulled a cup down from the cabinet and turned on the kettle.

"Morning," her parents said in unison.

Her father wasn't dressed yet for work, and her mother wore a light cotton bathrobe in cornflower blue. Both had half-drunk cups of tea in front of them. They were being awfully quiet.

"Dad, shouldn't you be at the garage?" Edna asked, glancing at her wristwatch. Her father was usually gone by now. She fixed her tea and sat at the table, glancing from her mother to her father, noting their gloomy expressions. "Who died?"

Her parents exchanged a glance, and it was her mother who said softly, "We have some news, Edna."

"Gosh, *did* someone die?" she asked, looking from one to the other. Her father did not look at her. They were acting so *strange*.

"No," her mother said.

There was that silence again.

"Well, come on, let's have it, Mother," Edna said. She sipped her tea, wondering briefly if she should have a piece of toast but deciding against it. She was anxious to get to her bed.

"Your sister is getting married," her mother said.

Edna nearly spit out her tea. "Getting married?" It was such a bizarre turn of events that she burst out laughing. "To whom? Don't tell me she's marrying that lowlife, Jerry Melvin." It'd be just like her sister to turn around and marry Jerry because Charley broke it off with her. She was so spiteful.

"No," her mother said quietly.

Although her parents seemed upset, this was good news for Edna. It meant that Edith would be moving out of the house.

"Well? Who's the lucky fella?" Edna wanted to shake the man's hand for taking on her sister.

Her father lifted his head, and it looked as if he'd been crying. "Charley."

"Charley?" she repeated, looking from her mother to her father, not understanding. She laid her hand over her chest, fingers splayed. "Charley next door?" She'd been about to say *my Charley* but caught herself in time. Blinking, she whispered, "No."

The expressions on her parents' faces confirmed her worst fear. She could feel all the blood draining from her face, and the room began to spin as her world crumbled.

She jumped out of the chair. "That can't be true! They aren't even seeing each other anymore."

Her parents were at her side. "I know it must hurt," her mother said.

"When's the happy day?" Edna asked sarcastically.

"Next week."

Edna's eyebrows knitted together. "What's the rush?"

"Because your sister is in the family way," her father said angrily.

"Edith is going to have a baby?" If it wasn't so serious, Edna would have laughed. Her sister couldn't take care of a plant, much less a child.

"But why Charley?" Edna said. She knew him to be an upstanding sort of person, but it wasn't his responsibility to make things right for Edith. Sometimes he was too good. None of this made sense to her. "Why doesn't she marry the guy who put her in the family way?" she demanded.

Her parents' silence answered all her questions. Of course—the only guy she'd been dating was Charley. Edna's posture sagged.

Oh, Charley. What have you done?

"She can't marry him. You have to stop it!" Edna told her mother and father.

"Don't be ridiculous, Edna. She has to. She can't be having a baby without a husband," her mother said.

Edna could no longer feel her legs. She began to sway, and she knew she was going to hit the floor but she could not stop it. The strong arms of her father wrapped around her and led her gently to the chair. Edna broke down in sobs. She put her head in her hands and continued to cry.

This couldn't be happening. It just couldn't!

Edith and Charley getting married? The two of them were going to have a baby!

A sharp pain started in the center of her chest and radiated out to her shoulders and belly. It took her breath away. For a moment, she wondered if she was having a heart attack. People dropped dead from heart attacks all the time. She almost welcomed the idea, thinking of the relief death would bring.

But soon the feeling was replaced by an anger that welled up within her, ready to explode. Her sister had caused her unfathomable pain. *How could she?*

"I'm going to strangle her with my bare hands," she said through gritted teeth.

For the next few days, Edna kept to herself. She stayed in her room, only leaving it to come down for meals and to go to work. She picked up every available shift at the answering service. Although the circumstances of her sister's wedding tempered any enthusiasm, wedding plans were still discussed, and she did everything she could to avoid those conversations.

The plan was for Edith to move next door and live with Maloneys. Mr. Maloney was fixing up a room in the basement for them. In the meantime, Laura helped Edith pack up some of her belongings, and Edwin carried the few boxes over to the house next door.

Edna's parents were at a loss for words around her. They didn't know how to comfort her. Both were angry with Edith, but that wouldn't last forever. She was their daughter, too, after all. Edna's father, whom she was always close to, couldn't even speak about it without tearing up. So Edna said nothing. Kept her emotions in control around him.

One beautiful sunny afternoon as she lay on her bed in a funk, disinterested in the weather and everything else, there was a tentative knock on her door. It couldn't be her parents; her father always did a quick rap and her mother usually knocked and peeked her head around the door.

"Come in." She didn't have the energy to lift her head off the pillow.

The door opened slowly, and Aunt Lenore appeared.

"Hi, Aunt Lenore." Edna did not sit up.

Aunt Lenore had always been a favorite of Edna's. She was so sensible and despite her own heartbreak over the death of her husband years earlier, had created a life for herself and her son, Johnny. Edna always thought her aunt was someone to be admired.

Lenore approached the bed. "May I?" she asked, indicating a free space on the side of the bed by Edna's feet.

"Wait a minute." Edna sat up and swung her legs off the bed, sitting on the edge of it, her hands leaning against the mattress on either side of her.

Her aunt sat down. She wore a simple shirtdress in navy and her brown hair, now streaked evenly with gray, was cut short and had a bit of curl to it. She wore a pair of clip-on earrings.

"How are you, Edna?" Lenore asked softly.

With that, Edna burst out crying, and Lenore put her arm around her and pulled her close until Edna's head rested against her shoulder. Her aunt smelled of something floral, light and comforting.

"That's a good girl. Let it all out. You've been hurt greatly," Lenore said.

Edna sobbed for a good bit until she felt as if she had not another tear left in her body.

Finally, she sat straight up and sniffled. She stood and retrieved a handkerchief from the top drawer of her dresser and blew her nose vigorously. She resumed her space next to her aunt, her shoulders slumped. All that crying had made her feel worse.

"What has happened is awful, Edna. And you're going to feel terrible for a long time."

Edna swallowed hard and nodded. She was afraid of it, this awful feeling of wishing her life would end.

"I can't believe it," Edna said. Another round of crying began again, but she soon stopped and wiped at her eyes with her handkerchief.

Her aunt's forehead creased with sympathy and concern. "Have you spoken to Charley?"

Edna shook her head. "No. I haven't even seen him." That wasn't entirely true. From the upstairs window, she watched him leaving every morning to go to work and returning in the evening. She thought she might be imagining the sagging of his shoulders, but she was sure he didn't look like someone about to be married. He looked more like someone facing the gallows.

"Charley's a nice boy. He's probably a little embarrassed about the recent events."

Edna snorted. "I'll say."

Gently, her aunt asked, "Have you spoken to Edith?"

Edna responded with a pronounced shake of her head.

"You can't ignore her forever."

That was exactly what she planned to do. "We've never gotten along. Not even as children. We're antagonistic toward one another."

"Your mother and I were so very different when we were younger. As we got older, we grew closer," Aunt Lenore said.

Sister or not, Edna could not picture growing closer with Edith.

Her aunt continued to speak. "But Laura and I managed to put our differences aside and forgive each other the wrongdoings that occurred."

Edna knew the story, how her mother's boyfriend at the time had murdered Lenore's husband.

"How did you ever forgive my mother?"

"I won't lie—it took a long time. I blamed her for John's death. For bringing that awful man into our lives. But in the end, it wasn't Laura who killed my husband. It was Horace. Now, looking back, I can see it was the right thing to forgive her. Had I not forgiven her, I wouldn't know you, wouldn't have been there while you were growing up. And I'd never give that up. Plus, you and Johnny were always so close."

Edna was glad her aunt had forgiven her mother, because she couldn't imagine Aunt Lenore or Johnny not being in her life. All the major holidays were spent at her aunt's house.

"Someday," Lenore said, "not today and most likely not tomorrow, you're going to have to find it within you to forgive Edith, to forgive both of them." When Edna snapped her head up, her aunt nodded and said firmly, "Yes, Charley is as much to blame as Edith."

Not sweet Charley. The only one to blame here was her sister.

"You can't drag this around with you for your whole life," Lenore said. "You're going to have to figure out how to make peace with this terrible thing."

Edna looked at her aunt, unblinking. "I'll never forgive Edith. Not as long as I live."

Chapter Eighteen

Edna dreaded the upcoming nuptials down at City Hall. Wished it was all behind her. But more than anything, she didn't want to go and bear witness to it. How could she stand there and watch while the love of her life married her sister? If only there were a way out. She had begged her mother and father to let her give it a miss, but they wouldn't hear of it. Even her father insisted that she go in a show of family unity. Her mother reassured her that the actual ceremony would only be ten or fifteen minutes, and then they were all going back to the Maloneys' house for refreshments.

The night before the wedding, Edna tossed and turned, unable to sleep. In a moment of desperation, she found herself, after midnight, standing outside on the grass between their two houses and throwing pebbles at Charley's bedroom window, hoping the sound woke Charley and not his brother.

After the fourth pebble hit the glass, Charley's younger brother, Danny, stuck his head out the window. Edna shrank back into the shadows against her own house. But it was too late; she'd been spotted.

"For crying out loud, Edna, what are you doing?" Danny said into the darkness.

"I need to talk to Charley. Wake him up."

Danny's head disappeared and Edna waited. She walked around to the front yard. The crickets were loud, and the sound of a train in the distance roared through the night, its whistle mournful. The front door opened and Charley appeared, yawning, rubbing the back of his head, wearing a T-shirt and striped pajama bottoms.

"What's wrong, Edna? Is everything all right?" He bounced down the steps, his feet bare. "Is it Edith?"

Edna shook her head. "Edith is fine. Sound asleep."

"What is it then?" In the light cast by the moon and the streetlamp, she could see his sleepy smile. "What's so important that you had to wake me up in the middle of the night?"

"I have something to tell you," she started. Her mouth was dry, and her hands shook.

"You couldn't do this during the day?" he asked, but his tone was jovial. He wasn't someone who was prone to impatience.

She shook her head. "Charley, I need you to listen to me."

"I'm listening."

"I love you."

He narrowed his eyes slightly as if not fully understanding the crux of the conversation. "I love you too, Edna. We've been best friends forever."

She shook her head quickly. "No, no, I mean I'm in love with you. I have been for a long time. I've always loved you. There is no one else for me but you."

"Edna—"

"You need to know this before you marry my sister. I can't love anyone else but you."

"Edna, don't say these things. You'll only regret them," he said kindly.

She wanted to scream as frustration mounted inside of her. Why couldn't he see what was obvious and so right?

He reached for her, touching her arm. "Your turn will come soon enough, and you'll forget all about me."

Something inside Edna died as it dawned on her that it was really going to happen. The wedding of her sister and Charley was like an out-of-control locomotive, and it couldn't be stopped. Although she felt like jumping in front of it. She balled her fists at her side.

"Go back to bed," he said. "We've got a big day tomorrow." He chucked her gently on her chin. He began to walk back to his porch. She watched him.

He stopped and smiled at her. "Don't worry, we'll always be friends, Edna."

"Will we?" she asked softly.

"Of course."

Somehow she couldn't imagine hanging out with Edith and Charley once they were married and had a place of their own. Edith wouldn't go for that one bit. At that moment, she knew that not only had her dreams been dashed, but her lifelong friendship with the boy next door was over.

The following morning dawned sunny and warm. Edna stood behind her parents as Edith and Charley were married before the justice of the peace. Several times during the ceremony, Mrs. Maloney looked over at Edna with sympathy.

Not once did Charley look at her or even glance in her direction. Not once did he say anything to her except "Thank you" when she congratulated him after the wedding. It was almost as if he was ashamed to look at her, and that made Edna want to die.

It was the most painful day of her life.

Maybe, she concluded, some things were better left unsaid.

Weeks later, Edna watched from the front window as Charley arrived home from work, his coveralls dirty, carrying a metal lunchbox at his side. He walked toward his house, his head hung low, looking every bit like a condemned man walking to the scaffold.

She stepped out onto her front porch, the screen door slamming behind her.

"Charley."

He hesitated, his gaze bouncing back and forth between his own house and Edna's, before coming to stand at the base of her porch steps.

"Edna," he started, but she held up her hand. He went quiet.

"Will you answer one question for me, Charley?"

He nodded.

"Do you love her?"

His voice was so low it was barely audible. "Yes, I think so."

"Is she really pregnant?"

His face and the tips of his ears went the color of puce. "Yes."

Edna drew in a sharp, ragged breath.

"Did she throw herself at you?" Edna demanded. She wouldn't put anything past her sister, but Charley . . . *Oh, Charley, how could you?*

"It doesn't matter if she did or didn't or what I did or didn't do," Charley said softly. He didn't look at her. Couldn't look at her. "Because it's done." The last sentence he said with some firmness, indicating it wasn't up for discussion.

There were some things in life you had absolutely no control over, outcomes that could not be changed. This was one of those things. But the way it affected the trajectory of Edna's own life was numbing.

The screen door of the Maloney house opened, and Edith appeared, wearing an apron over her capri pants and sleeveless blouse. In her hand, she held a dishtowel. Domestic Edith was a new beast altogether.

Edith threw a hand up and said, "Hello, Edna!"

"Hi," Edna replied flatly.

"Charley, honey, your dinner's on the table," Edith said.

Charley turned beet red, and Edna clenched her teeth. Hearing her sister use a term of endearment for *her* Charley was like nails on a chalkboard. In a loud enough voice so her sister could hear, she said, "Edith has learned to cook in the last week? My, my, wonders never cease."

Charley lowered his voice so Edith wouldn't hear. "No, my mother does the cooking. Edith dishes it up." He grinned, and there was a conspiratorial twinkle in his eye. For a brief moment, he was the old Charley.

A lump so huge appeared in Edna's throat she thought she might choke on it. Her sister was living her life—the life she'd dreamed of, with the man she'd dreamed of.

Her sister had hijacked her future and taken it for herself.

Abruptly, she said, "Goodbye, Charley."

And she turned and went back inside the house.

Chapter Nineteen

For the next month, Edna kept busy working every shift offered at the answering service. Sometimes, she worked the four-to-eight and then stayed and worked the midnight-to-eight shift as well, continuing to squirrel away money. Though she hated the job, work was the one place she wouldn't run into either Charley or Edith. Their spur-of-the-moment wedding had the whole town talking, and in the beginning, conversations would stop when Edna took her seat at the switchboard. But she didn't care; it wasn't like they knew of her love for Charley.

It pained her that Charley and Edith continued to live right next door. Her sister was a terrible saver of money. Had Charley married her instead, they'd be in their own apartment by now. She didn't run into him anymore as he seemed to be avoiding her. She often watched for him from an upstairs bedroom window, hiding behind the drapes. Every time she saw him, going or coming, it was like a little stab to her heart. The only man she wanted was permanently out of her reach.

It dawned on her that at some point, Edith and Charley would make an appearance at their house. They couldn't go on forever not coming over, especially with a new baby on the way. Now that the deed was done, her parents were over the moon to be grandparents. They thought Edna didn't know of their joy, but she'd overheard their conversations, the excitement and the anticipation at the arrival of a new baby and the plans that were being made. She wasn't sure how much more of it she could take.

One day, she walked over to Pearl Street to see her Aunt Lenore and her cousin, Johnny, who was home from Chicago. She was eager to see him and hear about his new teaching job.

Aunt Lenore's boarding house was looking well. She'd used her inheritance from her parents' estate to reinvest in the big house. There was a new roof, and all the bedrooms had their own bathrooms now. The house bore a fresh coat of paint: plum with cream trim.

Lenore answered the door and broke into a big smile at the sight of Edna. She pulled her niece into a warm embrace.

"It's good to see you out and about," Lenore said.

"I hope you don't mind that I dropped by."

Her aunt gave her hands a gentle squeeze. "Not at all. You're always welcome here, Edna. You know that. Come on back to the kitchen, I need to take a pie out of the oven. Johnny went to town to get bread. I don't know how I missed that on my grocery list."

Edna followed her through to the back part of the house, breathing in the ever-present scents of Murphy Oil Soap and cake. It was odd to see her aunt working alone in the kitchen when for years, her housekeeper, Hilda, had been there. But the woman had been elderly and she'd passed away the previous year. Edna knew her aunt missed her. Currently, Aunt Lenore had a girl coming a few days a week to help with the cleaning and the cooking.

"I was about to make some tea, will you have some?" Lenore asked over her shoulder as she donned oven mitts and pulled a steaming pie from her oven.

"Sure, I'll have a cup." It wasn't like she had anywhere to go. Her evenings were now free for the rest of her life.

Lacking energy, Edna sagged into a chair at the kitchen table. The walk over had taken more out of her than she thought it would. It wasn't even that hot out.

Lenore hummed a little tune under her breath as she filled a teapot with tea leaves and added boiling water. She carried it, along with two china cups, over to the table. She placed a strainer over one of the cups and poured the steaming-hot amber liquid, then did the same for the other.

She handed a cup to Edna and pushed the creamer and sugar toward her, then sat across from Edna at the small table. "How are you doing?" Lenore asked, taking a swallow of tea.

Edna shrugged. "I don't know how I'm doing. The shock has worn off but I'm, I'm . . . I don't know what I am."

"It'll take some time."

Edna felt compelled to confirm what she already suspected. "You know how I feel about Charley?"

Lenore nodded. "I do."

"Did Mother tell you?"

Her aunt shook her head. "No, I figured it out myself."

"How?"

"You always speak of him, and you spend a lot of time with him, or you used to," Lenore explained. "And whenever he was around, your face lit up."

Edna nodded. "I have a favor to ask you, Aunt Lenore."

Lenore leaned forward and then back, waving her hands out. "Anything, Edna. Name it."

Edna laughed. "You don't even know what I'm going to ask."

"It doesn't matter."

She drew in a big breath. "I was wondering if I could let one of your rooms." If she was to survive everything that had happened, she needed to move out of her parents' house. Although it was unusual for a young woman not to live with her parents until she was married, it wasn't unheard of. Her current living situation was untenable.

Her aunt didn't hesitate. "Of course. I actually have one tenant moving out at the end of the month. It's the smallest room in the house, though."

Edna knew exactly which room her aunt referred to. "It's perfect." She was so relieved she thought she might cry. She had an option. For the first time in recent memory, she broke into a genuine smile.

"Of course, you wouldn't have to pay anything. You're my niece," Lenore said.

Edna put her hand up and shook her head. "No, Aunt Lenore. I'll pay my fair share like anyone else or I won't take the room." That she was sure of. She wanted no charity.

Aunt Lenore pressed her lips together. "We'll talk about it later."

They heard the front door open and the familiar whistle of Lenore's son, Johnny. This immediately brought a smile to Edna's face. When he appeared in the kitchen doorway, he grinned and set the grocery bag on the counter before turning and holding his arms open for his cousin. Edna went to him, still smiling, and let herself be hugged by one of her favorite people.

"How are you, cuz?" he said. "I'm so glad you're here. I was going to walk over to see you tonight."

The three of them sat down, and Johnny peered over at the cooling apple pie. "Could we get a slice of that, Mother?"

"Not yet, Johnny," she said. "It hasn't cooled down properly. But I have a coffee cake if you'd like that instead."

"Sounds great."

Lenore handed him a teacup, which he filled before topping up the other two. She then handed out plates of coffee cake and sat down.

After swallowing a large mouthful, Johnny said solemnly, "I heard about Edith and Charley. What a shock."

Lenore's eyes widened and she said hastily, "No need to fan that fire, it's already a blaze."

"How do you like Chicago?" Edna asked, hoping to steer her cousin onto another topic.

"I love it! It's an exciting city. There's so much going on. You're never bored there."

Edna knew that this was a fear of Lenore's; that Johnny would love it so much he'd never come back. She supposed she wouldn't want her only child living so far away either.

"How's your teaching job?"

"It's great. I love it. I'm teaching at a high school in the city."

"He's going for his master's degree at night," Lenore said proudly.

Edna felt a pang of envy for his life. It sounded exciting.

"Mother says you're at the answering service," Johnny said.

Edna nodded and took a bite of her coffee cake. She hadn't thought she was hungry, but this was delicious.

For the first time since everything had happened, Edna had a moment's peace sitting there with her aunt and cousin.

"Edna's going to move in here with me," Lenore announced.

Johnny looked at her in surprise. "You are? That's great."

"Your mother was kind enough to let a room to me. It's best if I get out of my house."

Johnny scraped the last bit of crumbs from his plate with his fork. "You should come to Chicago."

"Chicago?" she repeated as a jolt of possibility blasted through her.

"Sure. Forget about everything here. A change of scenery." Johnny looked over to the coffee cake on the counter. His mother, reading the cue, stood, took his plate, cut him another slice, and handed it back to him.

"Thanks," he said.

"But . . . but what about work?" Edna said.

He shrugged. "You've got job experience. Your mother says you're a good worker. One of the teachers at my school has a brother who's a supervisor at Bell Telephone in Chicago. I could put in a word for you if you like."

Although she didn't like working at the answering service, she was experienced. It was the only thing she knew. Her head spun. Here was another option. But a better one because it provided an exit.

"But where would I live?"

"With me, of course. I've got to move out of my own apartment as my roommate is getting married. Three's a crowd and all that." His laugh indicated no hard feelings. "Anyway, I've been hunting for a one-bedroom apartment, but I can look for a two-bedroom if you're serious."

Edna made up her mind, right there on the spot. "I am very serious. I want to do this." She turned to her aunt and said, "I'm sorry, but I won't be taking that room after all."

Chapter Twenty

Edna's parents weren't happy about her decision to move to Chicago. She hadn't expected them to be. But once Johnny had put the idea into her head, she could think of nothing else. Until now, the idea of leaving Lavender Bay had never occurred to her. But it was much better than ruminating over Edith and Charley.

It was a lifeboat, and she was happily and quickly climbing into it.

"It's too far away," her mother complained.

From her father came this: "Young, unmarried women do not go off and live in big cities. Not if they care about their reputation."

"I love you very much, but I need to go away," she told them.

"In time, all of this will fade," her mother promised.

She didn't think so. Her heart had been rent in half. No amount of time would be able to put it back together. "There's nothing here for me anymore."

"We're here!" her father protested.

Edna looked down at her hands. "I mean as far as my future."

"Edna, honey, you're still young, you'll love again," her mother promised.

She didn't doubt that, but she'd never love anyone the way she'd loved Charley. That part of her was broken. Some things got smashed beyond repair.

Her parents finally relented, reluctantly giving her permission to go. She shared her plans with them, how Johnny had secured a two-bedroom apartment in the city and how she had an interview at the phone company the following week. Her mother helped her pack. When the suitcase was closed, her mother said to her, "Remember, this is always your home, and when you get tired of Chicago—and you will—you can always come back."

"Thank you, Mother."

Her mother and father floated the idea of meeting with Edith before she left. "To patch things up," her father said. They were so insistent that she agreed if only to change the topic of conversation. She suggested the morning of her departure. But she had no intention of seeing her sister or speaking to her ever again. She wanted to be spared that smug expression of Edith's, knowing she'd run her sister out of town.

The day before her departure, when her mother was asleep after working the midnight-to-eight shift and her father was at the garage, she splurged on a taxi to take her to the train station, where she changed her ticket and sent a telegram to her cousin to inform him she'd be arriving a day early. Normally careful with money, she didn't flinch at the extra expense of cab fare or a telegram, thinking it was the price she had to pay to avoid her sister. Before she left the house, she took one last look around, a lump gathering in her throat. She left a letter tucked in an envelope for her mother and father. She shook off the threatening melancholy, turning her thoughts to her new life in Chicago.

Edna sat with Johnny on the stoop of their apartment building. Living in a building with a lot of other people was taking some time to get used to. Growing up in his mother's boarding house, Johnny was better used to the arrangement. Her cousin was like the older brother she never had. He spent the first weekend showing her around the neighborhood where they lived. He took her down to the corner grocery store, and he showed her where to get the train, pointing out the big board that showed her where to get off for her new job at the telephone department. It was all so strange. Chicago was on Lake Michigan, another one of the Great Lakes, like Erie back home but much bigger. In the beginning, Edna found the city very strange. There were so many people, and of all different nationalities, even in their own apartment building. She joked more than once that it was like the United Nations. The apartment next to them was occupied by a large Italian family, and the wonderful smells of garlic and frying meatballs not only made her mouth water but reminded her of her mother's friends the Ruggieros, and all the Sunday pasta dinners they had at their house. The apartment below was occupied by a Hungarian couple who spoke no English. Edna waved at them if she saw them in the common hall, which always resulted in a grin from the old man and a scowl from his wife.

"I got a letter from my mother today," Johnny said.

"How is she?"

He took a drag on his cigarette. "She's fine. She had some news, though." He scratched the side of his head with the hand that held the lit cigarette.

"I hope it isn't bad news."

He sighed. "I don't know what it is." He looked at her. "Edith lost her baby."

There had been no secrets between her and Johnny. Aunt Lenore had already told him that Edith and Charley *had* to get married. And one night over too many glasses of wine, right there on the stoop, Edna had confessed to her cousin how she felt about Charley.

"Oh." She didn't know what to think about that. She'd been expecting a red-haired, blue-eyed baby to show up on the scene, a baby who'd look just like Charley. The thought that that baby was no longer imminent confused her. Then she had a dark thought: Was her sister ever really pregnant at all?

She wondered how Charley felt about the loss of his baby. Relieved? Sad? Stuck? The familiar irritation of tears threatened, and she blinked several times to shove them away. Looking up, she was surprised to see that the night sky wasn't as starry as the one back home. The Lavender Bay sky on a clear night had millions of stars. She'd thought all skies were like that. Johnny explained it was due to the pollution.

"Will you go back to Lavender Bay now?" he asked. He lit another cigarette. She wondered if Aunt Lenore knew he smoked.

His question took her by surprise. "Go back to Lavender Bay? Why?"

"I mean, now that there's no baby . . ."

She frowned. "Baby or no baby, Charley is still married to Edith."

"People get divorced every day."

Edna snorted. "Not in Lavender Bay." She picked up her bottle of Coke from the step and finished the remainder in one gulp. There was only one thing she was sure of, and that was that Charley was lost to her forever.

Six months passed, and Edna was beginning to settle down in Chicago and get used to her surroundings. She and Johnny took turns shopping and cooking and cleaning the apartment. She even had a favorite butcher; it meant another two-block walk, but she didn't care. She liked her job at Bell Telephone. It was nothing like the answering service back home. She worked as an operator, answering calls. She liked the people she worked with.

She was surprised when a man from work asked her out on a date. She didn't feel any particular way about him, but she thought, *Why not?* Her cousin dated a lot, but it looked like he had no intention of settling down. That was all right; she was beginning to think that marriage was overrated anyway.

She and Johnny spent time together going to the movies, the beach, different restaurants, but they always found their way back to the mom-and-pop diners, where they relished roast beef and mashed potatoes or Edna's favorite, meatloaf. When Johnny got season tickets to Wrigley Field and the Chicago Cubs, Edna accompanied him when he was between girlfriends or when a girlfriend didn't like baseball.

She had her own formula for her social life: no more than two dates per week and if they started getting serious, she called it off. Even if she felt a strong attraction for the guy, she still ended it. Made some excuse. There was a part of her that was empty inside, and she suspected it might always be that way.

Chapter Twenty-One

1962

On her day off, Edna took the bus downtown to do some Christmas shopping, treating herself to lunch at the Woolworth's counter. The colorful decorations and all the lights added a festive air to the busy city. She loved it. She lingered at department store windows, taking in the holiday tableaux. They had nothing like this back home. There were store decorations all right, but nothing like these fabulous scenes. Some places played Christmas music, and she hummed a carol as she walked along. She and Johnny were throwing a holiday party on Saturday night for some of their respective work colleagues, the ones they considered friends. Mentally, she went over her list of all the things she needed to do. She couldn't wait. She'd even splurged and bought a new Christmas album, *The 4 Seasons Greetings*.

She would not be going home for the holidays. Her parents and Aunt Lenore had been out to Chicago at different times to visit, but Edna hadn't been back to Lavender Bay since she left. Johnny had been torn about leaving her behind over Christmas, but finally, at her insistence, he'd booked a train ticket, reassured that she'd accepted an invitation to Christmas dinner at a colleague's house. She'd been promoted to supervisor at Bell, and it was a job she took seriously and did well.

Snow began to fall as she rounded the corner of her street, burdened with bags, and she smiled. She liked snow at Christmastime, although in her opinion, once the holiday was over, you could have it. Thank goodness she'd stopped at the thrift store on the way home and found a good winter coat for herself.

As she approached her apartment building, she noticed a man sitting on the front stoop, hunched over, huddled into his coat, hands in his pockets, shivering. Edna froze. She'd recognize that form anywhere.

Charley.

The sight of him here, outside of Lavender Bay, caught her off guard. It amazed her that after all this time, her response to seeing him was still the same: Her heartbeat ratcheted up and her skin felt tingly. For a moment, she wondered if something had happened to her sister. She drew in a deep breath, steeling herself for the encounter, and walked purposefully toward him. She couldn't avoid him forever.

She stopped directly in front of him. "Charley."

His head snapped up and he jumped up from the stoop. "Edna."

"How long have you been waiting here?"

"About two hours."

"You must be frozen. Come inside, I'll make you a cup of tea," she said easily, as if she'd only seen him yesterday.

Charley took her bags from her and followed her up the steps, waiting for her to unlock the front door. They started up the two flights of stairs toward the third-floor apartment she shared with her cousin.

"Why don't you use the elevator?" he asked with a nod toward the birdcage-style lift in the corner.

"I've had the misfortune of being stuck not once, but twice in that deathtrap. So no more for me."

She unlocked the door to the apartment. The space was bright thanks to the large living room windows, which meant that even when the sky was gray and snowy, like today, they could keep the electric bill down by not turning on any lights.

"You can set those bags there near the table," she said, pulling off her hat, gloves, and coat and laying them on a chair.

He set the bags on the floor and slowly removed his coat and pulled off his hat. As he did, he looked around the place, taking in the cream-colored walls and the second-hand furniture upholstered in shades of gold and green. A television with a pair of rabbit ears occupied one corner, with the current issue of *TV Guide* perched on top of it. In the other corner stood a record player. Next to it, on the floor, was a metal rack lined with vinyl albums.

He'd put some weight on, she noticed. He looked more solid than she remembered.

She filled the kettle and turned on the stove. "Charley, would you like tea or coffee?"

"Coffee if you have it."

"When did you start drinking coffee?" she asked, poking her head out of the galley kitchen.

"On the job. It's what all the guys drink. It seemed easier."

That was Charley. Always going with the flow, never making any waves. Well, not never.

Once the coffee was made, she called out, "How do you take it?"

"Black."

She made a face. "Yuck," she whispered, and added two teaspoons of sugar and a liberal dose of Coffee mate to her own cup and carried them to the living room, where she set them on coasters.

"I'm sorry I don't have any cake or cookies," she said. They didn't keep that stuff on hand. As it was, she was using too much sugar in her coffee and tea.

"That's all right, Edna."

She took a seat on the sofa, pulled the glass ashtray closer to her, and opened a drawer in the coffee table, pulling out a pack of cigarettes. She was a social smoker, usually pawning a cigarette or two when she was out. But now she felt the need for one, telling herself that this would constitute a social occasion.

She leaned back, one arm crossed over her body beneath her bosom, the other propped up, holding the lit cigarette.

"I didn't know you smoked," Charley said quietly, settling into the easy chair across from her.

How would he? She hadn't seen him in years. She was going to say something smart, but instead, she gave a little shrug. She took a drag off the cigarette, turned her head slightly, and exhaled, a long plume of blue smoke drifting up toward the ceiling.

"What brings you to Chicago?" she asked. Her curiosity was getting the better of her.

He held his mug of coffee in both hands, sipping from it.

"Edith and I are getting divorced," he said.

"Why?"

He shrugged. "It's what she wants. You know your sister."

Edna chortled. Charley's parents were devout Catholics; they wouldn't be too thrilled with this news. It was as she'd once suspected—it hadn't taken long for her sister to tire of Charley. She was surprised it had lasted this long. Through the grapevine, she'd heard that they were still living with the elder Maloneys and that Charley had given Edith a mink stole the previous Christmas. Marriage had not matured her sister.

Edna leaned forward and tapped an ash off her cigarette into the ashtray. She took another long drag and set it down in the ashtray, a thin stream of smoke floating upward. She sipped from her coffee cup.

Frankly, she was at a loss. The air was filled with the sounds of muted traffic outside the window. Mrs. Sanders in the apartment below had the volume up high on *As the World Turns.*

"Charley, I don't understand why you came all this way to tell me this," Edna said.

Charley set his mug down on the coffee table. "I'm—" His voice cracked, and he coughed and cleared his throat. Looking down at the old carpet on the floor, he said, "I made a mistake, Edna." He gave a desperate little laugh. "Even my mother told me I should have married you instead of Edith."

Edna blinked several times. Edith must have loved that. She picked up the cigarette, tapped off the elongated ash, and took several puffs in quick succession before stubbing it out. For a long time—years—Edna had thought of Charley every day. But then as time passed and she moved on with her life, there were days when she didn't think of him at all.

"Did you ever love Edith?" she asked. She had to know.

He drew in a deep breath. "I tried. I really tried." He leaned forward, elbows on his knees, hands clasped. "In the beginning I think I did. I like to think I did."

Understanding dawned on Edna. If Edith couldn't be the star of the show, or the center of Charley's world, she wouldn't want to be in it. There should be some satisfaction in this for Edna, but if anything it made her depressed. So many lives ruined.

Charley went on. "The night before our wedding, you told me you loved me."

Edna felt the heat rise to her cheeks. She looked down at her lap. "That was a long time ago." She lifted her head and looked out the window, all that hurt rushing back to her.

"Do you still feel that way?" he asked.

She answered his question with one of her own. "What is your purpose for coming all the way to Chicago?" she asked.

"To fix the mess I made. I have a pretty good idea why you left Lavender Bay, and for that I'm sorry." There was a lengthy pause, and Edna waited.

"I'd like to start over," he finally said. "With you."

Edna startled. She couldn't be more surprised if he had asked her to fly to the moon with him. He couldn't be serious. Five years had passed. She studied him for a moment, realizing he was serious. But then things were always pretty straightforward in Charley's head. She should be flattered that he'd traveled all the way from Lavender Bay to Chicago to tell her this. That took some chutzpah.

"What does that even mean? What are you saying?" she demanded.

He was quiet. "It means whatever you want it to mean. I hope it means salvaging our friendship. I've missed that, Edna. I've missed *you*. Maybe it could mean that there's some kind of future for us down the road."

Did she want that?

"I'll come to Chicago," he said. "I know you've got a life here. I'll go wherever you want. I know I've hurt you, and I'm willing to do whatever it takes to make it up to you."

"I forgave you a long time ago, Charley," she said quietly.

There was a glimmer of hope in his eyes. She pitied him.

"Please, give me a chance," he said.

He was so earnest. She felt nothing but overwhelming sadness.

She couldn't look at him, choosing instead to pick an imaginary piece of lint off of her skirt. "I can't. I'm sorry."

He sagged in the chair, deflated. "Edna, you cared for me once..."

"I loved you. I never stopped loving you."

"Then what's the problem?" he asked, looking every bit as confused as she felt.

She blew out a long breath that seemed to come from the depths of her soul. "The problem, Charley, is Edith and the fact that you married her. Regardless of the circumstances, you chose her *first*. And if there's one thing I know about myself, it's that I have no interest in my sister's castoffs."

As soon as the words were out of her mouth, she stood, not looking at him. She did not want to see a wounded look on his face. What she wanted was for him to be on his way. She picked up her coffee mug and the ashtray and carried them to the small kitchen. He had no choice but to follow her.

"Edna, please," he said behind her.

She shook her head. "No. I'm sorry you came all this way for nothing."

"It wasn't for nothing."

She picked up his coat and handed it to him. "The thing is, I've moved on with my life. I had no choice."

He looked at his hat in his hands, the muscle along his jawline ticking. He made one last attempt. "We could make it work. I'm not saying it would be easy, but we could be happy."

She had nothing more to say on the topic. "If you hurry, you might be able to catch a train in time to get back home late tonight."

He nodded and slowly pulled on his coat. She walked him to the door. As she put her hand on the doorknob, he pulled her into his embrace and squeezed her tightly. "Let me love you, Edna."

"Charley, let me go," she said quietly.

Without looking at her, he let her go and slipped out the door. She closed it behind him, put on the chain lock, leaned against it, and broke down crying.

Chapter Twenty-Two

1969

Dear Edna,
Mother and Dad have told me that you're moving back to Lavender Bay. They're very happy about this. It'll be good to have you home again. I'm glad you're coming back and I hope we can put the past behind us.
Safe travels,
Edith

"Are you sure about this?" Johnny asked her. His face was all scrunched up with concern and worry.

Edna smiled. "I've never been so sure about anything in my life."

"I don't want you to feel like you have to leave because I've bought a house," he said.

"No, it isn't that," she said. "I've been thinking of moving back to Lavender Bay for a while now."

"Really?"

"Uh-huh," she said with a nod. "I miss it. I miss everyone." *Except Edith.* She hadn't responded to her sister's letter and had no intention of doing so. Her parents weren't getting any younger and after almost ten years in Chicago, she was ready to return home.

"I've got three bedrooms in this new house," Johnny tried again.

"And one of them's got my name on it?" she said with the lift of an eyebrow.

Johnny laughed that wonderful laugh of his. She was going to miss him and their easy friendship so much.

"Thank you for everything, Johnny," she said.

Her cousin winced. "You're not going to get all sappy on me now, are you?"

"Yes, I am, and you're going to listen," she said firmly. "You saved me during a very dark time in my life."

He rolled his eyes up to the ceiling. "Now I'll have a savior complex."

She laughed and elbowed him. "You're like a brother to me."

"And you're like a sister to me," he said. "When are you leaving?"

"I'd like to help you get settled in your new home."

"I'd like that. You know how hopeless I can be," he said.

She nodded. "I know, but those of us who love you wouldn't have you any other way."

"That's great then. Do your parents know you're coming home?"

"They do. I called them last night. Apparently, my room is ready and waiting, just as I left it." Her father had started crying on the phone when he heard. It made her realize all the drama had been hard on them too.

Edith had remarried shortly after her divorce from Charley. All Edna knew about Edith's new husband was that his name was Bill, he worked in an office, and her parents liked him. As for Charley, the last she'd heard was that he'd moved up to Buffalo, married a girl from there, and at last count had two kids. Edna was happy for him. He'd moved on.

Johnny's new house was in a leafy suburb of Chicago, a tidy redbrick bungalow with a concrete driveway and boxy shrubs out front. Edna helped him move, and they went furniture shopping together at the thrift shop. She advised him not to spend his hard-earned money on new furniture at this point, to simply pick up some second-hand pieces until he got situated. She'd bought him a houseplant, an impossible-to-kill variegated ivy, which would be well suited to her cousin because she was pretty sure he'd forget to water it. She made a note to call him to remind him.

Before they unpacked his boxes, they painted the walls and cleaned and organized his kitchen and bathroom cabinets. At night, they sat on moving boxes and ate takeout pizza and drank a few beers.

At the end of the week, Johnny took her to the train station. Everything she wanted to bring with her, she managed to get into two suitcases, donating the rest of her things to the thrift shop. She'd start fresh in Lavender Bay.

She was so proud of her cousin and all he'd accomplished, going for his PhD and now teaching at the college level. She hugged him goodbye, anxious to get on the train and get home. Ready to start the next chapter in her life.

It was raining when the train rolled into Lavender Bay. Edna looked out the window with hungry eyes, wondering if she'd still recognize it. The train station hadn't changed at all. Still the same small redbrick building with a second-story clock tower. Even the stationmaster looked the same, except his hair was now snow white. Her parents were waiting for her inside. She hugged them both.

"We are so happy you've come back home," her mother said with tears in her eyes.

"Nothing's been the same since you left," her father said. He couldn't stop staring at her, as if he couldn't believe she was actually standing there in front of him in Lavender Bay.

She linked arms with her mother, and her father took the heavier suitcase. Edna carried the other one with her free hand. They hurried to the car, trying not to get soaked, and her mother got into the front seat as her father loaded the suitcases into the trunk. Cars went by, red taillights in the darkness of a rainy day. There was the constant swish of spraying rain from moving cars.

In the back seat, her gaze went back and forth from one side of the street to the other, taking everything in, noting with satisfaction that nothing had changed in her hometown. She sat back with a smile on her face.

It was good to be home.

Her father carried her suitcases upstairs to her old bedroom. She and her mother followed him up.

"It's so good to have you back," Laura said.

Over his shoulder, Edwin said, "I never thought you would come home!"

"I missed Lavender Bay," Edna said truthfully. Though she'd certainly miss Johnny. He'd been a great friend to her over this past decade.

Her room was just as she had left it. The maple bedroom set, the twin bed, the dresser and the bureau. The bed was covered in the familiar green chenille bedspread.

"I almost redecorated this room," her mother said as her father set her suitcases down in the middle of the floor.

"You could have, Mother," Edna said. It was their house after all.

"We'll let you unpack and get settled. Then come downstairs, we've picked up a cake from the bakery."

"Sounds good. Give me a few minutes."

"Take your time," her father said. He couldn't stop smiling.

"Edna, would you like tea or coffee?"

"Tea's fine, Mother."

Her parents left and Edna hoisted her suitcases onto the bed, unsnapping the latches and popping them open. She carried her bras and underwear over to the dresser. When she opened the top drawer, there was an envelope inside with her name on it. She recognized the delicate penmanship of her sister.

With a grim set of her lips, she pulled the cream-colored envelope out and arranged her undergarments in the drawer. She left the drawer half open and sat on the edge of the bed, leaning against the maple footboard. With a heavy sigh, she pulled out the sheet of paper tucked inside the envelope.

Dear Edna,
Welcome home!
I can only hope that we can patch things up and have a sisterly relationship. Looking forward to talking to you soon.
Love
Edith

She reread Edith's short letter. Her sister must have been smoking something if she thought that just because Edna had been gone for ten years, she'd forgotten the events that drove her away in the first place. She crumpled up the letter and the envelope and tossed them into the black metal trash can in the corner.

Nothing had changed for Edna with her return to Lavender Bay. As far as she was concerned, her relationship with Edith remained non-existent.

Chapter Twenty-Three

Edna was out one day walking around town, searching for a gift for her father's birthday. She'd always been close to her dad, and she wanted to get him something special. She'd even told her mother she'd make the frosted banana cake that was his favorite. She had been home for two months, and while in many ways it felt as if she'd never left, she had noticed that her parents were slowing down. Almost sixty, her mother was talking about retiring from the answering service, and her father was thinking of selling the garage. His back and neck hurt, and he didn't know how much longer he could do the work.

Although Edna's mother had encouraged her to come back to the answering service, Edna had been in no great hurry to get a full-time job. She'd saved quite a bit when she lived in Chicago, between the good money she'd made working at Bell and her thriftiness, which was now becoming legend—she was a regular at the second-hand shops and had never met a sale she didn't like. Instead, she surprised everyone, including herself, by enrolling in a business course at Lavender Bay Business School, taking typing, shorthand, bookkeeping, and stenography to make herself more marketable. For a bit of income and a way to keep busy and get out of the house a few nights a week, she'd taken a part-time bartending job at Dog Days Bar.

She slowed as she approached the Quirk and the Quill, a new card shop that had opened while Edna was in Chicago. It was housed in a small, narrow space that had once been a barbershop. The red, white, and blue pole still hung out front.

The Quirk and the Quill was owned by Loretta Jablonski, who was the daughter of Alistair and Harriet Young, former boarders at Aunt Lenore's boarding house, so Loretta was practically family. But Loretta wouldn't be there that day, having given birth to her first child the previous week.

Thinking she might find a card for her father, Edna went inside. Her footsteps echoed on the old wooden floor, and she nodded to the teenaged girl behind the counter who was holding down the fort. A transistor radio played "Suspicious Minds" by Elvis Presley. She began to search through the cards in earnest, debating whether to get him a funny card or a thoughtful one. She was standing there, card in hand, laughing, thinking she might go with a humorous one after all, when she was approached by a fellow customer.

"Hello, Edna."

Still laughing, Edna looked up and came face to face with Edith. Her smile immediately disappeared. In the ten years since she'd last seen her sister, she hadn't changed much. Her auburn hair was in a stylish updo, and there was heavy black eyeliner on the lids of her sharp green eyes. She was dressed smartly in a two-piece pink outfit: a dress that went to her thigh and a matching coat. On her feet were dark pink shoes with a square toe. It seemed a little excessive for a card shop, but then Edith always had a sense of fashion about her.

"How are you?" Edith asked, her eyes searching her sister's face.

Edna put the card back in the rack, turned on her heel, and walked out of the shop without saying a word.

1971

Edna fiddled with the strap of her handbag as she waited in the reception area of the Gibson's Grape Jelly factory. She'd applied for a secretarial job after spotting a help wanted posting in *The Lavender Bay Chronicles*. She glanced around the room, trying not to be disheartened by the fact that there were quite a few other women there, all of them younger. It hadn't occurred to her that she might be too old for the job. Maybe they'd prefer someone younger, someone who was more trainable.

Although she'd had decent grades in school, Edna had never been college-bound, that much was certain. But the year at the Lavender Bay Business School had been a wise decision. She'd enjoyed it, she'd become proficient in some marketable skills, and it had boosted her confidence. When she lived in Chicago with her cousin, they used to talk about how important it was to keep finding ways to improve and educate themselves. Once she finished business school, she turned to the high school, which had started continuing adult education courses. On her last phone call with Johnny, she'd told him about the course she was taking on car maintenance. He'd agreed with her take on things: she had no husband or brother, therefore she should learn how to change a tire and check the oil.

She was thinking about such things when her name was called. She jumped out of her seat, dropping her handbag, its contents spilling out all over the floor. Horrified, she knelt and gathered up a compact, a change purse, two lipsticks, keys, a used tissue, half a pencil, a pen cap whose pen had long ago vanished, and half a pack of gum that was so old the remaining pieces were stuck together. Hurriedly, she shoved them all back into her handbag. Edna stood, brushed off her knees, and smiled at the woman who waited patiently for her to pull herself together. She was aware of the stares of the other job applicants locked on her as she walked away.

The woman who stood waiting for her in the doorway carried a pile of manila folders in one arm. She thrust out her other hand, which was small and feminine and whose short nails were painted a coral color. "I'm Penny Joyce. I'm head of the secretarial pool."

Edna was impressed. This other woman wasn't that old, and she already had a good position here at the jelly factory. She supposed it helped that the factory was run by a woman.

Penny was about the same age as Edna and was smartly dressed in wedge heels and a brown print dress with a matching sash and large pointy collars. Edna looked down at her own outfit, something she'd picked up at the thrift shop, and thought she looked kind of frumpy. There was nothing she could do about it now. At least everything was clean and ironed and there were no runs in her nylons.

She followed Penny, who walked briskly ahead of her. Penny stopped halfway along the corridor, opened a door, and beckoned Edna inside with a warm smile.

It was a conference room done up with walnut furniture and orange accents. With her brown dress and copper hair, Penny appeared to be a color-coordinated accent herself.

"Please take a seat anywhere, Edna," Penny said.

Spotting the pile of papers at the head of the long conference table, Edna took a chair on the side closest to the pile.

Penny made herself comfortable in the chair at the head of the table. She went through the pile of papers to her left and pulled out Edna's application. Briefly, she glanced over it before lifting her gaze and smiling at Edna.

"I see you're a recent graduate of Lavender Bay Business School."

"That's right," Edna said. She sat straight up, her back rigid, hands on the clasp of her handbag.

"And what's your WPM?" she asked.

Getting down to business right off the bat, Edna thought. "When I left school, I was clocking in at seventy-two words per minute."

"Very good. We require our typists to do a minimum of sixty. Would you still be up at that speed? You graduated a few months ago."

Edna nodded, her posture relaxing slightly. "I love typing. I practice at home." She'd picked up a used typewriter at a garage sale. Once home, she'd discovered that some of the keys were stuck, but a little dab of mineral spirits on the type bar below the ribbon cover had fixed that.

Penny looked at Edna's application again. "And you've taken shorthand, dictation, and some bookkeeping."

"I'll be honest and admit that bookkeeping isn't my strongest suit," Edna confessed.

Penny smiled. "I appreciate your honesty."

Edna lifted one shoulder in half a shrug.

Penny frowned. "It also says on your application that you work part time at the Dog Days Bar?"

"That's correct," Edna replied. "I needed something when I returned from Chicago, and that filled the void."

"I must ask, and pardon me if it seems rude, but do you drink yourself?"

Edna chortled. "Oh goodness no. I enjoy the odd glass of wine now and then, but I'm not a drinker." True, she and Johnny had shared cocktails and bottles of wine, but that was in Chicago. Since she'd been home, she hadn't had so much as a single tipple. But she still smoked the odd cigarette.

"Currently, we are looking for three women to complete our typing pool," Penny said. "Once I go through all the applicants, I'll decide on a few, and then Miss Gibson will interview the remaining candidates."

This surprised Edna and she didn't hide it. "Really? I would have thought Grace—er, Miss Gibson—wouldn't be bothered with something like that."

"Miss Gibson is pretty much hands-on with everything around here. And she likes to meet all the new hires."

Edna was impressed.

Penny stood, indicating the interview was over. "Thank you for coming in, Edna. If we're interested, we'll be in touch."

Edna shook her hand and headed out the door. As she passed the waiting room full of younger women, she felt as if all the air had leaked out of her. By the time she arrived home, she'd concluded that she probably wouldn't hear from the Gibson's Grape Jelly factory again.

A week later, Edna sat at the kitchen table of her parents' house, going through the help wanted ads again. The only typing position available was in Cheever at the old aviation plant, which had been converted into a factory that made glass tubes for televisions. Did she feel like driving twenty miles back and forth every day? She didn't think so. One of the drugstores in town was looking for a stock clerk, and she supposed if she couldn't get a typing job, she could apply for that. Having the job at Dog Days gave her some room to maneuver. She'd wait a bit and see if any other ads popped up.

She was in the middle of making herself another cup of coffee when the phone rang. She picked up on the third ring.

"The Knickerbocker residence," Edna said.

"May I speak to Edna Knickerbocker, please," said a female voice.

"This is she."

"Hello, Edna. This is Penny Joyce from Gibson's Grape Jelly."

Edna perked up. "Yes?"

"Would you be willing to come in for an interview with Miss Gibson?"

"I most certainly would," Edna said.

"Would tomorrow morning at ten work for you?" she asked.

"Yes, that'll work just fine." There was no need to consult her appointment calendar. First, she didn't have one; and second, she was free all day, every day, until she had to go into work at the bar. But that was in the evenings.

"Very good, I've penciled you in and we'll see you tomorrow."

"Thank you," Edna said, and she hung up.

The following morning, Edna wore her smartest outfit, the one she kept for weddings and funerals. This job interview was as important as any of those. It was the only outfit in her closet that hadn't come from a thrift store, a dark green affair she'd purchased at one of the department stores in downtown Chicago. She paired the matching skirt and jacket with beige shoes, a blouse that had a fussy tie at the neck, and a pair of small gold clip-on earrings.

She left early, borrowing her father's car. And it was a good thing, too, as there'd been an accident out on the highway and it delayed her. She arrived at the factory with only moments to spare.

As she walked through the parking lot, she took some deep breaths, glancing at her wristwatch every few seconds to make sure she was still on time. With one minute to spare, she announced herself to reception, where three women sat behind a long, curved desk, answering phones and greeting visitors.

Immediately, she was led to the top floor, which seemed to house all the offices. The young woman from reception, whose name was Cindy, walked quickly, her high heels clicking a rhythm along the industrial tile floors. They passed the room occupied by the typists, where Edna spied approximately ten desks. The sound of clacking keys and the ding of the return carriages brought a smile to her face.

The young woman stopped at a thick walnut paneled door, which bore a brass nameplate reading *Miss Grace Gibson, CEO*. That made Edna smile as well.

Cindy rapped on the door and opened it when a "Come in" was issued.

Edna followed her inside, unsure of what to expect.

Grace Gibson immediately stood from her partners desk. Behind her was a wall of windows. From where Edna stood, all she could see outside was the sky, with clouds interrupting the vast blue.

Grace approached and thanked Cindy, who exited the room, closing the door softly behind her.

Grace Gibson was dressed smartly in a Chanel suit. The only reason Edna recognized it as such was because Edith had worn one at a recent family funeral and had bragged about it to their mother at the luncheon afterward.

Edna shook Grace's offered hand.

"Edna, it's so good to see you again," Grace said.

She smiled in response. "It's good to be here."

They walked toward Grace's desk, and Grace indicated that Edna should take a seat in one of the guest chairs in front of it. Once she was situated in her own chair behind it, she said, "I can't tell you how delighted I was to see your name among our applicants."

Edna felt that boded well.

"So you want to come and work at Gibson's," Grace said.

"Very much so."

Grace opened a manila folder in front of her and leafed through the few papers there. From her side of the desk, Edna could see her own application. She raised an eyebrow slightly, hopeful that having her own folder might signify something positive.

"You worked for Bell Telephone in Chicago," Grace said, eyes on the papers in front of her. "You were there for almost ten years and were promoted to supervisor. I see you've brought two letters of recommendation with you from your superiors at Bell." Here she looked up at Edna.

Edna was unsure if a response was required. But Grace continued, "What did you like about working at Bell?"

The question caught Edna off guard. For a moment, she blinked and said nothing, but finally managed to pull her thoughts together. "I liked the work, and I liked the people I worked with. All different kinds of people. It was interesting."

Grace nodded. "One of your supervisors reports that you never missed a day."

"I liked working," Edna said. That much was true. She'd liked Bell so much more than Block's Answering Service that she never minded going into work. Plus, earning her own money gave her a sense of satisfaction and independence.

"Reading your education history, it seems you've been busy in your spare time."

"I think these continuing adult education courses they offer at the high school are a great idea."

Grace smiled as she read some of Edna's courses: "Automobile Maintenance, Growing and Canning Your Own Vegetables and Fruit, Macrame, Ceramics . . ." She looked at Edna. "You've covered a nice variety of subjects."

Edna was about to launch into an explanation of how she was a big believer in self-improvement, but remembered she was here with the hopes of securing a job and didn't want to toot her own horn, so she said simply, "Thank you."

"I'd love to offer you a position in the typing pool, Edna. It's Monday through Friday, nine to five, and it pays one hundred and fifteen dollars a week."

"Thank you!"

"Would you like to think about it and get back to us?"

Edna shook her head. "No, I'll take the job."

"That's wonderful. When can you start?"

"I can start tomorrow morning if that's all right with you," Edna said.

"That's perfect."

They discussed a few other items related to her employment and when Grace stood, so did Edna, reaching out to shake her hand and thanking her. She walked out of the jelly factory smiling, her head held high, excited at the prospect of a real job again.

Chapter Twenty-Four

1975

Edna continued to work as a typist at the Gibson's Grape Jelly factory and had recently been promoted to typing pool manager, a position she was proud of. Two to three nights a week, she tended bar over at the Dog Days Bar. Aside from the occasional mean drunk, she liked the company and the music playing on the jukebox, and it had turned into a social outlet for her. Now closer to forty than thirty and with no interest in getting married, she'd accepted the fact that she would have no children. It was too late for that.

After years of living at home with her parents and building up her savings, she managed to purchase a house of her own over on Sandy Lane, within walking distance of the bar. Her parents were sorry to see her leave, but it was time. She soon had her own routine and despite everything, or because of it, she could honestly say she was content.

She continued to avoid her sister, however. It was easier once she moved out of her parents' house as prior to that, she'd arrange to leave if she knew Edith was coming over. Her parents begged and pleaded for the two of them to reconcile, but Edna wouldn't hear of it.

Dear Edna,

I wanted to share with you that I'm getting married to Herb Bermingham next year. I'd like very much for you to attend. And I think Dad and Mother would like that as well.

Herb is quite a bit older than me, but I think he's perfect! Third time's the charm I guess.

Edith

"Her optimism never ceases to amaze me," Edna muttered as she tossed the letter into the garbage can.

Edna stood behind the bar, drying glasses with a dish towel. Outside, there was a torrential downpour. The rain felt steamy and offered no real relief from the scorching summer heat that had preceded it.

A man about her age pushed through the door, soaking wet. He shook himself like a dog, rainwater going everywhere. She narrowed her eyes at him. She'd never seen him before. As a near-lifelong resident of Lavender Bay, Edna knew everyone and everyone knew her.

As he approached the bar and heaved himself up onto a bar stool, he let out a long sigh.

Three stools away, Jerry Melvin held out his empty beer glass for Edna to refill.

"Edna, when will you say yes and marry me?" Jerry asked. "So I can make you an honest woman."

Edna laughed. "I'm already honest, so your proposal is unnecessary."

He didn't seem too perturbed by her refusal, and his face lit up when she pushed another glass of beer toward him. She turned to the other man, who seemed like he had the weight of the world on his shoulders. He looked as if he might have played football once. Although short, he had the physique of an offensive lineman. He had sharp eyes and sandy-brown hair that was beginning to gray at the sides.

"Can I help you?" she asked, sliding a paper coaster toward him. On the front of the coaster was an advertisement for Genesee Beer.

"A Genny please," he said without looking at her.

"Draft or bottle?"

"Bottle's fine."

She set the drink in front of him, and he reached for his wallet.

"No need," she said. "You can pay when you're finished."

"I'm only having one."

She smiled. "Are you sure?"

He nodded, lifting the bottle to his mouth and taking a big gulp.

"Tough day?" she asked.

"Yeah. You could say that. I've got four kids at home and they're driving me nuts."

"I can imagine how your wife must feel," she said smartly. Here he was having a beer and she was probably stuck at home with those kids who were driving him nuts.

He looked at her, not smiling. "I don't know how my wife feels. She's over in the cemetery."

Edna blanched and tried to remove her foot from her mouth. "I am so sorry."

He brushed her apology away. "No need to apologize. How would you know?" He thrust his hand over the bar and mustered a smile. "My name's Hal. Hal Grimsby."

She shook his hand firmly. "Edna Knickerbocker."

"Don't mind me, Edna, grumpy isn't my normal state."

With his wife gone and four kids underfoot, she thought he'd be allowed to be grumpy on a regular basis. "Don't worry about it. Hold on a minute, Hal, I've got to put the hockey game on."

She walked over to the far corner of the bar, where a television sat up on the shelf near the ceiling. She pulled out a stool, climbed up on it, and turned on the game, adjusting the volume so everyone could hear but not so that it was too loud.

"Do you like sports, Edna?" Hal asked when she returned.

"I do, actually. Although hockey is my favorite," she told him.

"Really. Why's that?"

"Because I'm a terrible ice skater, so I really admire anyone who can play a sport on skates, much less stand up on them."

Hal laughed. "Fair enough. I prefer baseball myself, though if I'm honest, if I had the time, I'd follow all the sports—baseball, football, basketball, hockey, you name it."

She supposed being a single parent didn't allow much free time. Not that she felt sorry for him; he wasn't a "woe is me" type of person.

"Are you a Braves' fan?" she asked of Buffalo's basketball team.

He nodded. "The Bills, the Braves, the Sabres. Now if we could just get a baseball team!"

"From your lips to God's ears," Edna said.

The door to the bar opened. The rain had stopped. She recognized Hugh Campbell coming in with a friend.

"Hugh, would you mind leaving the door open?" she said. The air was stifling inside and she hoped a breeze might find its way in and offer some relief.

Hugh Campbell, tall and dark-haired, took the doorstop, a black ceramic cat that weighed a ton, and set it against the open door. It had always amazed Edna that with all the shenanigans taking place inside the bar, the cat hadn't ended up broken.

Hugh and his friend sidled up to the bar. "Two Gennys, please, Edna," he said.

Edna eyed his sandy-haired friend in his plaid cotton short-sleeved button-down shirt. "And who is this?" She made it her business to know everyone in town.

"This is Martin Cook, a buddy from college."

Edna nodded in acknowledgement. "Welcome to Lavender Bay, Martin. Where are you from?"

"Utica."

"Never been there."

She handed them their beers and looked around to see if anyone needed anything. At the far end of the bar, Hal finished his beer. She approached him and asked if he wanted another.

He shook his head. "No thanks. I've got to get home. I left my fourteen-year-old in charge. It was nice meeting you, Edna."

"You too, Hal. Take care of yourself."

Hugh called her over. "Hey, Edna, can I ask you a favor?"

"It depends," she said. Hugh was a good kid, but she didn't want to sign her house over or anything like that.

"Where does Gail Sturges hang out? Does she come in here?"

Edna chortled. "Not on your life." The Sturges were a nice family. She'd babysat Gail and her sister, Louise, quite a bit when they were young. She'd even taught them how to swim. She eyed Hugh and noted the dewy-eyed optimism in his face. She liked Hugh. She liked Gail. She leaned toward him conspiratorially, elbows on the bar. "From what I understand, a lot of the kids in Lavender Bay go up to the disco in Cheever."

Hugh looked surprised. "They do? It's so far away!"

Edna gave him a look that read *What do I know?* She nodded to Martin. "What's your story?"

"I just finished grad school and I'm looking for a job."

"You got a girlfriend?"

He shook his head and then with a grin, he added, "I'm hopeful."

Edna cackled. She decided she liked Martin too.

"Edna!"

The three of them turned in the direction of the voice. Jerry Melvin lifted his empty beer glass. "Come on, Edna, another drink, please."

With a sigh, she muttered, "Coming, Prince Charming."

Hugh and Martin burst out laughing. As she walked away, she heard Hugh say, "I guess we're going to Cheever tonight."

"That's great. You said Gail has a sister?" Martin asked.

Edna smiled to herself. She went to the other end of the bar and got Jerry another beer. It would be his last one, though. He'd had enough and was prone to turning surly. She'd call his brother and tell him to come and pick him up. When she looked up, she saw that Hugh and Martin were gone.

1981

Edna leaned against the back counter behind the bar, arms folded over her chest, and yawned. She stared at the clock on the opposite wall. Two more hours. She was dead tired. She hadn't slept well the previous night and had been at work all day at Gibson's. She wasn't twenty anymore. She wanted to go home and crawl into bed.

The bar was quiet tonight. The regular patrons were still recovering from New Year's Eve. Currently, there were two men sitting at the bar, arguing about the newly elected president, Ronald Reagan, although the inauguration was still weeks away. Obviously one of the men was a Republican and the other, a Democrat, but Edna wasn't worried; they were civil despite all the booze they'd consumed. She glanced at the clock again, hoping no one else came in so she could close early. As soon as these two fellas left, she'd start shutting things down. The boss wouldn't mind; he certainly wouldn't want to keep the lights on if there were no customers sitting at the bar to pay the electric bill.

Christmas lights were still on in the front window, giving the condensation that covered the glass a multicolored glow. Spray snow had been stenciled over the bottom half of the window. She was going to need a scraper to get it off. It was a job she did not cherish, and why she insisted on doing it every December was beyond her. No more, she told herself. Hoping the last two patrons would get the hint, she wiped down the bar and the sink. Then she grabbed the dish rag and a small metal bucket, walking around and wiping down the tables and emptying the ashtrays. After she had wiped down every table, she made the rounds again, wiping out the ashtrays with the rag. When she returned to the bar, the two were on their feet, throwing down dollar bills on the bar to cover their bill.

"Thanks, Edna," said the one.

"Goodnight, Edna," said the other, and they pulled on hats, coats, and gloves and walked out the door, still arguing over politics.

"Goodnight, fellas!" she said. As soon as the door closed behind them, she went to the back to get the mop and bucket. When she returned, there was a man standing in front of the bar. Her shoulders sagged. She should have locked the doors behind those other two when they left. She pressed her lips together.

As she neared the man, she said, "I'm sorry, I'm closing up." She crossed her fingers, hoping he wouldn't say anything to her boss. She didn't want to get into trouble, but she was bone tired and wanted to get home. Her alarm would be going off in six hours.

The man, who looked to be in his sixties, said, "I'm not here for a drink, Edna."

She froze. She did not know this man. How did he know her name? She swallowed hard. She'd read enough true crime to know that she might end up in a shallow grave somewhere. But he didn't look the way she'd expect a serial killer to look. He was clean shaven, smelling of expensive cologne and looking as if he'd just had his hair cut. He wore a London Fog trench coat and a pair of Florsheim shoes.

She narrowed her eyes. "Do I know you?" She leaned the mop against the front of the bar.

He smiled warmly. "No, we've never met." He extended his hand. His nails were well manicured, and on the ring finger of his left hand he wore a black onyx ring with a diamond in the center of it.

"Herb Bermingham," he said.

So this was Edith's third husband. Edith's ability to bounce back after a failed marriage never ceased to amaze Edna. She was made of some sturdy stuff. Edna shook his hand, not saying anything. There was nothing to say; he already knew who she was.

"It's nice to meet you finally, Edna. I've heard a lot about you," Herb said.

I bet, she thought. But instead, she said, "What can I do for you, Herb?"

He nodded toward a bar stool. "May I sit down?"

"Of course," she said. Abandoning the mop and bucket, she stepped behind the bar. "What will you have to drink?"

"A whiskey, neat, if it's not too much trouble," he said, making himself comfortable on the stool. He looked out of place there in Dog Days with his three-piece suit and trench coat. Like he'd walked into the bar by mistake. He had a country club feel about him, or a private men's club, not a second-rate bar in Lavender Bay.

"I've got Seagram's, Canadian Club—"

"Canadian Club is fine," he said.

Although she'd never laid eyes on Herb, she'd heard about him from her parents. He was the CEO of some manufacturing company and had a lot of money. He had grown children and had been a widower for years before meeting Edith at the golf course. Edna couldn't picture her sister swinging a golf club around; she didn't have an athletic bone in her body.

Edna poured three fingers of whiskey into two glass tumblers. She set the bottle of whiskey down and slid one glass across the bar to Herb.

He lifted his glass up to her and took a generous sip, pressing his lips together after he swallowed his drink.

"What brings you here?" she asked. The thought of going to bed had retreated to the back of her mind as curiosity overtook her.

"Your sister, actually."

Despite herself, Edna asked, "Is she all right?"

He smiled. "Edith's fine." She waited for him to give the reason for his visit.

"My first wife and I were married for twenty years," he said, tracing a finger along the rim of his glass. He stared at the whiskey and smiled.

Seeing that there was going to be a story, Edna pulled over a stool on her side of the bar and sat, biting back a sigh so as not to be rude. Snow began to fall lightly outside.

"We were very happy, and when she died, I was devastated," he admitted. There was a faint smile on his lips. He looked up at Edna. "I didn't think I could know that kind of happiness again. Until I met your sister."

The Edith she knew didn't spread cheer, she only left a trail of destruction behind her. She remained silent, wanting to hear more about this version of her sister.

"She is an amazing woman," he said. His expression told her that he truly believed that. Edna bit her tongue.

"At my age," he continued, "I didn't think I could be this happy again. When we got married six years ago, people said it would never last. My friends thought I'd lost my mind. My kids didn't speak to me, telling me I was about to make the biggest mistake of my life."

Edna finished her whiskey and poured herself another glass. She tilted the bottle toward Herb, but he shook his head.

"Anyway, your sister is such a delight—"

Here Edna snorted. She couldn't help it. Edith was many things, but a delight? Herb must be off his rocker.

He wasn't offended by her reaction and humored her with a smile. "I've gone on too much, I suppose." He was not apologetic about it. "I'll get to the point of my visit."

Edna gave him an encouraging smile. At the back of her mind, she hoped no one else walked through the door. To get up now and lock it would seem rude.

"Your sister's happiness is my number one priority," Herb said. "I was hoping to facilitate a reconciliation between the two of you."

He hardly had the words out of his mouth before Edna was shaking her head. "No, no, no."

"You won't even consider it?" he asked.

"No, I'm sorry, Herb. You seem like a nice man, and I hope Edith realizes how lucky she is," Edna said truthfully, "but too much time has passed." She reached beneath the bar for her pack of cigarettes and an ashtray. She tapped one out and offered one to Herb, who declined. Once she lit it, she took a long drag and asked, "Does Edith know you're here?"

"No, she does not," Herb said.

"Why not?" Edna asked, wondering if this was more his idea than her sister's.

He hesitated before answering. "I didn't want to get her hopes up. I couldn't bear her to be hurt."

How thoughtful.

"Look, Herb, you seem like a nice man, and I'll spare you the details of what happened between Edith and me but suffice it to say that to ask me to forgive and forget is asking the impossible."

Unoffended, he smiled genially. "All I could do was ask."

"It's allowed."

"Then I guess there's nothing more for me to say," he said. He stood from the bar stool, leaving his whiskey unfinished. "I feel sorry for you, Edna."

This infuriated Edna and she jumped off her stool. "I don't want your sympathy, Herb. You've delivered your message, and now you can go back to my sister. Good luck. You're going to need it."

She escorted him to the door, where he took his fedora off the rack and pulled it on before walking out.

"Goodbye, Edna."

She said nothing, closing the door behind him and locking it. She turned off all the lights to discourage anyone from stopping in and poured herself another glass of whiskey. She sat in the darkness of the bar, nursing her drink, unsettled by the visit.

Five years later, when she heard that Herb Bermingham had had a massive heart attack while playing golf and had died near the ninth hole, Edna lifted a glass of whiskey to him. Her fight had not been with him. He might be a poor judge of character in his choice of a wife, but he'd never done anything to her. After she finished her whiskey, she penned a short letter to Edith.

Edith,

I'm sorry to hear that Herb has passed away. I met him once and he seemed a decent man. He really loved you, that much was evident.

Now you know what it feels like to lose the love of your life. That much we now have in common.

Edna

She tucked the letter into a stamped envelope and set it in the top drawer of her dresser, thinking she'd mail it in the morning on her way to work. But when she woke up the following day, she pulled the letter out, ripped it up, and tossed it in the garbage.

Chapter Twenty-Five

1991

Edna had not felt this awful since the day she found out that Charley had eloped with Edith. Now she sat on the sofa huddled with her mother, who kept dabbing at her eyes with a lace-edged handkerchief, sniffling from time to time. The black hole inside of Edna, which had been getting smaller and smaller as time passed, was split wide open with her father's death. She stood at the edge of a precipice looking down into a dark chasm and saw that it was endless.

"I don't know how to go on without him," her mother said. And those words set off another round of crying. Her shoulders shook with each sob. She lifted her head and searched Edna's face. "How do we do this?"

In that moment, Edna no longer felt like the child, no longer felt like the dutiful daughter, but more like the adult. She looked at her mother's expression, a reflection of her own. Her mother looked as lost as she felt.

Edna slowly shook her head and said in a low voice, "I-I-I don't know." And she didn't. She couldn't imagine a world without her father in it. It was something so unfathomable it shook her to her core.

Edwin Knickerbocker had been unwell for some time. His symptoms had been subtle at first, and he'd been dismissive of them. Everything he ate bothered his stomach. His acid reflux was out of control. He drank Mylanta right out of the bottle. Then he began to have difficulty swallowing food like potatoes and rice. They'd be sitting at the dinner table, and his hand would go to his throat and he would lift his chin as if he were trying to facilitate moving his food down. Finally, Laura and Edna convinced him to seek medical help. But by the time the tests were completed, it was revealed that he had advanced esophageal cancer. Before his wife and daughters could process what was happening, he was dead. From the first appointment with the doctor to the morning he passed away in the hospital bed they'd set up in their living room was a total of six weeks. It had happened so fast that at times Edna still couldn't believe it. She'd always been closer to her father; he'd been her champion. No matter what, she could always depend on him. Not that she didn't love her mother, because she did, but Laura Knickerbocker's interests had always been more in line with Edith's.

And now, two months later, she sat on the couch with her mother, still crying.

The front door opened, and Edith entered. Her eyes were red-rimmed. Since their father died, she'd been a more frequent visitor, coming over to spend time with Laura.

"Hello, Mother, hello, Edna," Edith said. She set her purse on the rocker next to the television and sat down in the armchair, crossing her legs.

Edna made to get up, as Edith's arrival was always her cue to exit. But Laura grabbed her hand. "Don't leave, Edna."

Reluctantly, she remained seated next to her mother.

Laura looked from one daughter to the other. "Your father is dead and to my eternal shame, the two of you didn't patch it up before he died."

Edna felt her face go red and she burned inside. "What are you talking about? We kept the peace while he was dying."

Her mother flinched. "Yes, you did, and I was hopeful as was your father that maybe, just maybe, things had improved." Now she looked at Edna. "But as soon as the funeral was over, you resumed your previous behavior. You don't talk to your sister—"

Raising her voice slightly, Edna said, "I have nothing to say."

Laura spoke over her. "You leave the room when she enters it. This has gone on long enough. It's been over thirty years!"

This behavior was the norm now. They'd spent more time not speaking to one another than anything else. It was how it was.

Edith spoke up. "I've tried reaching out to Edna down through the years, but she wants nothing to do with me."

"I know," Laura said with a sympathetic glance at her younger daughter.

Was this how it was going to be? Laura siding with Edith? How Edna missed her father! Pain grew and ballooned inside of her, replaced by fury.

"It's all *my* fault?" she said.

"Really, Edna, don't you think it's time to let go of the past?" Edith pushed.

Laura put up her hand. "I can't go through all of this again. Not now. Dad is gone, and the two of you must try to get along. You must find a middle ground."

When neither said anything, Laura added, "Someday, I'll be gone, and you'll only have each other."

They all went quiet. Laura looked at Edna, who remained seated next to her. "What do you say, Edna?"

Edna was aware of both of them staring at her. But she didn't want to agree to anything in this vulnerable state.

She stood up and shook her head. "I don't know. I don't know." She left the room, and no one tried to stop her.

1994

That's it then, Edna thought as she settled the bill with the hotel for the funeral luncheon for her mother. Despite beating breast cancer twenty years ago, Laura had succumbed after a nasty bout of pneumonia. Up to that point, she had been in pretty good shape for her age. Edith was on the other side of the room, powdered and lipsticked, dressed in a Chanel suit, wearing black nylons and sensible pumps. She appeared to be holding court and had a small crowd surrounding her, most of them men. They were the type of men like Edith's third husband, men who golfed and had cocktails at the end of the day when they returned home from work.

Laura's sister Lenore was unable to attend the funeral. She had moved to Chicago years ago to live with Johnny and was now too old and infirm to travel. Johnny, of course, couldn't leave his mother alone so he, too, was absent that day. Edna was disappointed. She missed him, but she understood. The only family present was her and Edith. Their numbers were dwindling.

A couple of stragglers approached Edna as the luncheon wrapped up. They were women who'd worked with Edna and her mother at the answering service. She chatted with them for a few minutes, and they hugged her goodbye and left.

The last to leave were Laura's old friend Diana Sturges and her husband, Mark. Diana had been quite upset. But she appeared composed now and Mark guided her toward Edna, his hand on her elbow. Edith, smelling of Chanel No.5, came and stood on the other side of the elderly couple.

"Oh, girls, I am so sorry for your loss," Diana said with feeling. "I don't know where I'd be today without your mother. She was there for me at a very difficult time in my life. She and our friend Joy and I, we were like sisters." Edna and Edith exchanged a glance, and Diana continued. "I couldn't have asked for better friends."

"Come on, Diana," Mark said gently. "We should go and let the girls settle things."

Edna and Edith hugged the couple goodbye and watched as they left.

"I suppose we should pay the bill," Edith said, breaking the silence.

"I already took care of it," Edna replied.

"Oh. Well, what do I owe you? I'll write out a check for my half."

"Not necessary," Edna said. It was the least she could do for her mother: give all their guests a fine meal. And she certainly didn't need her sister's money, not when she had her own.

"Okay . . . thanks," Edith said.

They stood there together in a painful, awkward silence. Edna thought of other sisters. Sisters who shared an unbreakable bond, who were loyal, who loved each other fiercely, who had shared history. But that wasn't the case with her and Edith.

"Well, goodbye, Edna," Edith said.

"Goodbye, Edith," Edna replied.

Edith went to gather her coat and purse. Edna watched her walk away, wanting to call out to her, to say something. To say anything. But she froze, and the words wouldn't come.

Chapter Twenty-Six

1999

With great curiosity, Edna watched from her front window as a man about her age with two other men, whom she suspected to be his sons, judging by their age and by the familial resemblance, unloaded a U-Haul and carried furniture into the house next door. The house had sat empty for the past three weeks. She missed the previous owners, Ed and Marilee, a lovely couple. They'd been great neighbors since Edna purchased the house almost twenty years ago. She'd been there while they raised their kids and sent them off to college and was a guest, front and center, at all of their weddings, baptisms, and other family events. But that was all over now. She felt bereft. She'd miss their weekly Scrabble games and the cookouts and most of all, sitting in their screened porch out back in the summer, talking about anything and everything. Ed and Marilee decided they could no longer tolerate the long winters and had sold their house and moved to Florida, encouraging Edna to come and visit them. But Edna didn't like traveling. Everything she needed or wanted was right here in Lavender Bay. She knew she'd never make that trip to Florida.

She didn't know anything about the new owner other than that he was a widower. This disappointed her. She'd been hoping for another family, preferably with young kids so she could watch them grow up the way she'd watched Ed and Marilee's kids go from toddlers to college graduates. Lather, rinse, repeat. But it was not meant to be.

It took all day for the new neighbor to unpack. As the sun went down, he stood at the end of the driveway and waved his sons off as they pulled away in the U-Haul, presumably to return it.

For whatever reason, maybe because she felt loyal to Ed and Marilee, Edna kept her distance. She did not drop off a casserole or an apple pie as Marilee had done for her when she first moved in. Nor did she walk over or introduce herself. When she pulled out of her garage, she only waved if he waved first. She normally considered herself a very social creature, but maybe she was too old to make new friends or acquaintances. It felt like there should be a limit on that sort of thing once you reached a certain age. That was her thinking, anyway.

So Edna tooled along, minding her own business, doing the things she liked to do, enjoying the life of a retiree. When she'd hit fifty, she quit the bar and when she turned sixty, she retired from Gibson's Grape Jelly factory. Her free time was spent scouring garage sales and thrift shops for bargains was still one of her favorite hobbies, and from time to time, she emptied her own garage and attic. If the day was going to be sunny and dry, she'd set something out on her front lawn and put her asking price on a sign next to it, as she had that morning. Her old Schwinn bike, which she'd purchased back in 1970, had now seen better days. There'd be no more bike riding for Edna; the last time she'd done it, she'd fallen off and broken her arm. That was the end of that. So she propped it up on the front lawn, nearer to the sidewalk. For the sign, she'd cut a piece of cardboard from one side of a box and with a thick black Sharpie marker, had written *$15*.

She was on her way home from the thrift shop, pleased with her purchase, a perfectly good pink quilted robe similar to the one she'd worn herself back in the early seventies. A quick wash and it would be like new. She was anxious to get rid of the bike, and she hoped some kid would be sitting on her porch waiting for her to return. It had been a great bike, and she'd like to see someone else get some use out of it.

As she pulled her 1984 blue Chevy Impala into her driveway, she spotted her next-door neighbor deadheading his rosebushes at the front of his house. He waved and she automatically threw her hand up in response.

She got out of her car just as two teenagers walking along the sidewalk stopped and stared at the bike, shaking their heads.

"It's in great condition," she told them.

One of the girls scowled at her and said, "You're crazy, lady."

"There's no need for rudeness, young lady," Edna scolded.

Next door, she thought she heard laughter. She turned, and although her neighbor had his back to her, she could see his shoulders shaking.

Frowning, she walked over to the bike to make sure it was all right. It would be hard to sell a bike if it had a flat tire. But the tires were all right. It was when she straightened the cardboard sign that she noticed it. A zero had been added to her *$15* and it now read *$150*. She looked up and down the street until her gaze settled on the new neighbor, who was now laughing outright. Edna put her hands on her hips. "Ha-ha."

He crossed his lawn and stepped onto her driveway. "You gotta admit it was funny," he said.

"I admit nothing," she told him. Up close, she studied his features: aged, face weathered, gray hair that matched her own. But the unsettling thing was, he looked familiar.

"Hal Grimsby," he said, thrusting out his hand.

Edna shook it, her eyes never leaving his face. "Edna Knickerbocker."

"You don't remember me, do you, Edna? I recognized you as soon as I moved in," he said.

She shook her head. "I'm sorry, I don't. But you look familiar. Have we met before?"

He laughed. "You probably don't remember, but I came into Dog Days Bar . . ." He looked up, squinting, and said, "This was more than twenty years ago. I came in once because I was having a bad day with my kids, and I had one beer."

Edna clapped her hands and crowed, "Yes! I remember you. You never came back again. Your kids must have improved greatly."

He laughed. "Somewhat."

What a pleasant surprise that Hal Grimsby from so long ago was her new neighbor!

"Isn't it a coincidence that you moved right next door to me?"

Hal nodded. "Strange things."

They made small talk for a few minutes.

"Hope you're not too mad," he said, motioning toward the cardboard sign.

"Not at all," Edna said. "I like a practical joke as much as the next person."

"Then we'll get along fine," Hal said.

"We sure will."

She carried the cardboard sign into the house, forgetting about her thrift shop robe in the back seat of her car. Inside, she leaned against the door and had a good laugh. There was only one thing for her to do, and that was to get even.

The next morning, she found herself at Gloria's Gift shop. She'd asked around town about where she could get a gag gift and the consensus was Gloria's. She'd been there years ago, thought it was too pricey, and had never returned.

The owner, Gloria Jeraldi, was parked behind the counter, seated on a bar stool, looking at her phone. She was a woman in her seventies, stocky and with perfect auburn hair Edna always suspected was a wig. No one's hair could be that perfect, she thought. It always looked the same. Always. Never a strand out of place.

Gloria looked up at Edna, smiled, and said, "Welcome."

"Thank you."

"Are you looking for anything in particular? Or are you here to browse?" Gloria asked.

"I heard you had gag gifts," Edna said.

Gloria chuckled and nodded. "I do." She pointed. "There's a whole section at the back of the shop. If you need anything, let me know."

"Thanks," Edna said.

In the front section of the shop were the respectable gifts, like soaps and candles and housewares. But in the back, it was a whole different thing: shelves and shelves of gag gifts and long-forgotten toys that were no longer popular. Edna was there for an hour looking at everything, picking things up, examining them, and turning things over. There were whoopee cushions—something she hadn't seen in forty years and didn't know they made anymore—fart trumpets, plastic snakes that looked alarmingly real. She had a great time. But when she landed at the barrel of small squirt guns in fluorescent shades of orange, pink, green, and yellow, she almost cried with joy. She immediately picked a green one, thinking it was a perfect way to get back at that neighbor of hers. Smiling, she carried it and a whoopee cushion to the front of the store, thinking she'd save the whoopee cushion for a future opportunity.

Back at home, she spotted the neighbor out front, using a tweezer to remove Japanese beetles from his roses and plopping them in a Mason jar. He waved as she pulled in and she waved back, smiling to herself, thinking he was in for a treat.

Inside, she put her purse and bag on the kitchen table and pulled out the squirt gun. She removed the packaging and disposed of it. She turned on the tap and filled the squirt gun. Smiling, she palmed it and went outside and walked over to her neighbor's yard.

Hal stopped what he was doing, his Mason jar a third full with beetles. She did not want to know what he had planned for them.

"Whatcha doing there, Hal?" she asked.

"Trying to get rid of these pesky beetles, they're destroying my roses—"

She whipped out the squirt gun and squeezed the trigger, noting the shocked expression on his face as the stream hit him right between the eyes.

"Welcome to the neighborhood, Hal," she said with a wink, and turned and made her way back home. As she went, she heard a raucous round of laughter behind her and soon, she was laughing too.

And that's how the squirt gun wars of Sandy Lane got started.

CHAPTER TWENTY-SEVEN

2008

Edna glanced up at the clock. She had about fifteen, twenty minutes before she was due at Hal's house for dinner. It was his turn to cook this week, and he was making his famous barbecue hamburgers. She'd made orange Jell-O and thrown in a can of fruit cocktail as she knew it to be a favorite of his. He said it reminded him of his childhood. She settled in her chair, groaning at the creak of her bones when she sat. She picked up *The Lavender Bay Chronicles* to give it a quick glance-through before going next door.

As she turned the pages, she skimmed the paper, coming to an abrupt halt on the obituaries. "Oh no," she muttered, her forehead gathering in a crease.

Charley was dead.

She sank back in the chair, dropping the paper in her lap and putting her head in her hand. Once she composed herself and her hands stopped shaking, she picked up the paper again and read the obituary about the former Lavender Bay resident. All the pertinent information was there. Beloved husband of Debra. She raised her eyebrows when she saw all the children he'd had.

She counted out loud. "One, two, three, four, five, six, seven. My, my, Charley, you were busy!" But then she smiled, delighted that he'd had the big family he'd always wanted. Fifty years ago, she'd loved him more than anyone. Sometimes, she still dreamed of him, and she suspected that maybe you dreamt of lost loves because the love was still there. But with Charley, it was never meant to be.

Closing her eyes, she relaxed in her chair and let the memories, the good ones, wash over her. The paper slid from her hand and fell to the floor. The love she'd had for Charley when she was young had been fierce, full of passion and anticipation. She'd been swimming in hope. If she were to feel like that now about anyone, even Hal, who'd become her best friend, it'd probably kill her.

Her phone rang, startling her out of her reverie.

"Hello?"

"Edna, are you coming over? Dinner's ready."

"I'm on my way, Hal." She hung up the phone. She placed her hands on the arms of the recliner and pulled herself out of it, folding the paper neatly and setting it aside. It was time to get going. She'd picked up some almost-like-new Nerf guns from a garage sale that morning and she was anxious to try them out with Hal. She laid the Nerf guns on top of the bowl of Jell-O in the canvas bag and headed out the door.

Chapter Twenty-Eight

Present Day

For three days, Edna wrestled with the knowledge that her sister was in the hospital. Did her sister expect her to visit her? To start making decisions about her care? She hadn't a clue as to what Edith's wishes were. It was as if a total stranger had dumped a whole lot of responsibility in her lap.

She discussed all these things with Hal as they sat around her dining room table playing a game of Scrabble. The weather was miserable outside: damp and rainy. Hal always beat her in this game; he was a voracious reader. In the beginning she'd challenged words he laid down, thumbing through the official Scrabble dictionary in search of said word only to be disappointed. Now she didn't bother challenging him. Her preference was for card games of any kind. That would be next time. They used to play a lot of pinochle with another couple, but they had since died, which was a shame.

"Maybe she's not asking anything of you," Hal said, studying the board, his gaze swinging back and forth between it and the letters on his tray.

Edna snorted, waiting as patiently as she could for him to finish his turn. It always took him forever. On occasion, she'd remind him that it wasn't a championship tournament or that there was no money riding on the game. He'd just laugh and continue to take his time, explaining that he liked to challenge himself.

"Edith always has an agenda," she said.

Hal paused, switching his gaze from the board to her. "Can you say that with certainty? You've barely spoken to her in the last seventy years."

Edna shrugged, unwilling to concede the point. "People don't change that much."

Hal shook his head. "I disagree. People do change over time."

He didn't know Edith the way she knew her. She'd told him the whole story of what had happened all those years ago. His response had been "To be honest, he doesn't sound that wonderful if he chose flash over substance." Edna didn't speak to him for three days after that comment.

She wouldn't back down. "I think people can mellow with time, but change? I think the core remains the same."

Hal looked at her again. "Can you honestly say you're the same person you were at eighteen? Twenty?"

She thought about it for a moment. "Pretty much."

He shook his head. "I don't think I'd recognize my twenty-year-old self these days. Life is about personal growth." Hal read a lot of self-help books. He was always on the quest to better himself, whether it be personally or physically.

She gave it further thought. *Was* she the same person she was all those years ago? Granted, she wasn't the dewy-eyed Pollyanna she'd once been. "Well, I've had life throw me some curveballs that have affected me and possibly my outlook, but I'm still the same girl whose parents instilled in her a certain set of values and morals."

Hal tilted his head slightly. "Hear, hear. Well said."

She smiled. "Now come on, lay down your tiles. You've had enough time."

He grinned. "I've been distracted." He arranged his tiles on the board, added them up, and said, "That's eighty-four points."

"Eighty-four points?"

"I used all seven tiles, that's fifty points right there. You're welcome to check my math."

"No, it's all right."

He wrote the score down on a scratch pad. She didn't have to ask the score to know that he was clobbering her.

That was all right. The next time they played cards, she'd beat the pants off him.

"Now, getting back to your sister," he said, "here's my unsolicited advice: go and see her. Mend the fence." Seeing the look on her face, he added, "No one is saying you have to become best friends, but it requires a lot of energy to drag that hurt around with you all the time. It's time to let it go, Edna."

Maybe he was right.

In the end, it was curiosity that propelled Edna to the hospital the following day. Apprehension filled her as she hadn't had a conversation with Edith in a long time. What would they talk about? The weather was always a safe subject, she decided.

Edna hated hospitals. She knew too many people who'd gone in and not come out, her mother being one of them. And there was something about the air in hospitals—it was the same way with malls and airports—they seemed to suck the life right out of you. By the time you left, you were logy.

She checked in at the reception desk, where they gave her a stick-on visitor badge and her sister's room number. She took the elevator up to the fourth floor, where the cardiac unit was located. Slowly, she made her way to

Edith's room. She stood in the doorway for a moment before entering.

Edith looked old and frail in the hospital bed. Being one year older than her sister, Edna wondered if that was how she appeared to other people as well. She didn't view herself as old and frail. More like aged. Like cheese. Edith was staring out the window, dressed in a feminine quilted bed jacket with pink ribbon trim.

When Edna crossed the threshold, Edith looked in her direction. Her face remained neutral, and she appeared to be at a loss as to why her older sister was there.

"Hello, Edna."

"Edith, how are you feeling?"

"I'm fine. I had a small heart attack. I'll be going home in a few days."

"That's good," Edna replied, not sure what else to say.

With a slight nod of her head, Edith said, "There's a chair there, you can sit if you like."

"Only for a moment. I can't stay long," Edna said, establishing the rules of the game.

She made her way to the chair and sat down, but refrained from moving it closer to the bed. "What happened?" she asked.

"I woke up one night with terrible chest pain. I could hardly breathe. First I thought it was indigestion, but it didn't improve after I took some antacid, so I called an ambulance and they brought me here. They did all sorts of tests and said I'd had a heart attack."

"Oh."

"Do you have any cardiac issues? They asked me about our family history. Mother didn't. But didn't Dad have a pacemaker?" Edith clasped her hands beneath her chin. On her left hand, she still wore the wedding set from her third husband. The diamond solitaire was large, and the companion band of diamonds was thick.

"He did," Edna said. "No, I don't have any cardiac issues, surprisingly. I watch my cholesterol and take a little walk every day. I must take after Mother's side of the family."

There was nothing more to say about their family history, so they fell into a prolonged silence. After a bit, Edna could no longer resist asking the question that had been bothering her ever since she'd gotten the first phone call. "Why do you have me listed as your next of kin?"

Edith did not hide her surprise at the question. "Because you *are* my next of kin. You're my sister."

Edna almost argued the point but remembered her sister had just had a heart attack and it would be cruel to wind her up. She did something she rarely did: she said nothing.

After several minutes of silence, Edna stood and said reluctantly, "Well, I'm glad you're all right. But I must be going."

Edith leaned forward in her bed, reaching out for her. "Please don't go, Edna. There's something I really need to talk to you about."

Panicked and unprepared, Edna took a step back, edging toward the door. "I can't stay, I have an appointment," she lied.

Edith sagged against the back of the hospital bed. "There's so much we need to discuss."

"I don't want to revisit the past," Edna said.

"I understand why you're so angry I get it, but there's more to the story than you know."

"I know everything I need to know," Edna challenged.

Edith closed her eyes for a moment and sighed, frustrated. "I would like to clear the air before I die."

Edna scowled. "Oh, for crying out loud, Edith, you're not going to die. You just said you're going home soon."

Edith shrugged, her bony shoulders lifting the quilted bed jacket. "At our age, anything could happen."

Edna pursed her lips. If her sister was looking for absolution, she wouldn't find it with her. It wasn't Edna's job to make things easy for Edith. But she couldn't imagine Edith not being there. Their feud had been large and all-consuming, and Edna had invested a lot of energy in avoiding her younger sister at all costs. Looking back, it was practically a full-time job.

"I don't know, Edith," Edna said sternly. "We haven't spoken in seventy years."

"I know. That's why I'm asking now."

"Why didn't you ask me twenty years ago? Thirty years ago?"

Edith regarded her with a tired look. "I tried several times to reach out to you and reconnect with you. It was a no from you at every turn."

Edna had to concede her sister's point, but she was unable to verbalize that. "Look, I've got to go. I'm going to be late for that appointment." She needed to get out of there.

"Can you come back?" Edith asked.

"I don't know, Edith," Edna said, inching closer to the door. "I won't make any promises."

"All right then, thanks for stopping," Edith said as if Edna were an Avon lady dropping off her order of lipsticks. "But if you change your mind, there are things I'd like to tell you . . ."

"Again, I make no promises," Edna repeated. "Good luck with your health."

And she was gone.

Chapter Twenty-Nine

The visit to see her sister had left Edna unsettled. For two nights, she didn't sleep well. What could Edith possibly have to tell her after all this time? And would it matter? They were too old to revisit the past.

She said as much to Hal a couple of days later. "She wants to unburden herself, but I have no interest in that. It's not my fault she has so much guilt for what she did."

"This has been the chorus to your song for as long as I've known you," Hal said. She did not miss the disapproval in his voice.

"She thinks she's going to die and she wants to make peace."

"Edna, she said there's more to the story," Hal said sharply, "It would be bad juju not to make peace with a dying woman."

"She's not even dying," Edna said. She'd thought for sure Hal would be on her side. But she should have known better. Hal was a peacemaker. He played the role perfectly with his children and grandchildren. He gave them a lot of unsolicited advice, though she had to admit that his advice was usually sound.

"Even so, you have an opportunity here to make things right," he pointed out. "Unless, of course, you don't want to."

She hated when he did this. Turned things around and upside down, which made her question her perspective.

"Maybe this is how you identify yourself. As a victim," he said.

Anger bloomed within her. "I was a victim! By her nefarious deeds, I lost Charley forever. She trapped him into marriage by saying she was pregnant."

"Edna, you've said all this before, but maybe it's time to take an honest look at things. Charley wasn't as perfect and wonderful as you thought he was. He shares responsibility with Edith for what happened. Even though he admitted to you years later that he'd made a mistake, his choices were his own."

Edith opened her mouth to say something, but Hal held up his hand.

"Being wronged by your sister is a large part of your story," he said.

"I can't help what happened," she said defensively.

"I'm not saying you can. What I'm saying is, are you afraid that if you were to make peace with Edith, it would redefine you? Would you lose your identity as the wronged sister? As a victim?"

Hal asked too many difficult questions sometimes. He should have been a counselor.

She tried a new angle. "This is pretty black and white. She wants to unburden herself to make herself feel better."

"Maybe she does and maybe she doesn't. Or maybe she wants to square things with her god."

Edna doubted that; it couldn't be anything as admirable as that.

"Don't do it for her," Hal said. "Do it for yourself. So you can let go of this anger you've been dragging around for seventy years."

Edna was quiet for a few minutes as she gathered her thoughts. "I don't know. You've given me a lot to think about. I'll take under consideration everything you've said."

"That's all I ask."

For a second time, it was curiosity that sent Edna to see Edith in the hospital. The more she thought about it, the more she realized she wanted to hear what her sister had to say. She wanted to know if Edith was capable of taking responsibility for her actions.

Edith was still in the same private room. When they'd renovated the hospital, they'd transitioned all the two-patient rooms into singles. Edna wasn't sure about this. When she'd had her hysterectomy thirty-five years ago, the woman in the other bed had been a delight. They got on like a house on fire, and at least there was someone to talk to during the long, interminable day.

She was surprised to see her sister had a visitor.

"Hello, Edna," Edith said. "You remember Rose Campbell, don't you?"

"I do indeed," Edna said, marveling at how beautifully Rose had aged. Some women had all the luck.

"Mrs. Knickerbocker, how are you?" Rose asked.

"I'm fine, thank you. I heard you were back for a visit," Edna said.

"Came up with my mother and my kids for two weeks. It's been great being back," Rose told her. "I heard Mrs. B was in the hospital, so I thought I'd pop in and say hello."

"And I really appreciate you coming in, dear," Edith said.

Behind her, on the windowsill, was a vase of colorful flowers. Rose must have brought them. Edna didn't believe in store-bought flowers. That's what gardens were for.

"I better get going. I promised the kids we'd do something this afternoon. Our time here is winding down,"

Rose said. She looked from one sister to the other. "It was great seeing the both of you. Best of luck, Mrs. B."

"Thank you, dear," Mrs. B said. "Keep in touch."

"Will do."

Once Rose left, Edna approached her sister. Her color was certainly better than it had been at the last visit.

"You came back," Edith said.

"I did." Edna moved the chair from the window up a few inches closer to Edith's hospital bed. Today her sister wore a floral bed jacket in shades of green, pink, and purple.

"I'll be going home the day after tomorrow," Edith said.

"That's good. How are you feeling?"

"Better."

Edna didn't think she could stand any protracted silences, so she said, "Why don't you tell me what you want to tell me."

"I see you're still very blunt," her sister replied. There was no judgment in her voice; it was more of an observation.

"It's who I am."

"How did we let things get so out of hand between us?" Edith asked.

Edna wasn't sure whether she wanted an answer or whether it was a rhetorical question. If they were going to be discussing questions that were more geared to the philosophers, she should have sent Hal instead. But since her sister had asked, Edna decided to answer.

"You destroyed my life, and you destroyed Charley's life as well," she said.

Her sister flinched at the words, but it wasn't Edna's job to sugarcoat things.

"I loved Charley with all my heart," Edna continued. "We'd been friends for so long, I was sure marriage between us was the next logical step."

With a sigh, Edith said, "I know."

"Then why did you do it? I know we fought a lot, but did you hate me that much?"

"Of course not."

"Then why?"

"I had been seeing Jerry Melvin. He was such a jerk. And after I broke up with him, Charley seemed sweet on me. And, well, he was so different from Jerry that I got swept up in it. He was so nice, and I wasn't used to that. Jerry was a lot of things, but nice wasn't one of them."

"I'll say."

"Charley was always the perfect gentleman."

"He couldn't have been too perfect, considering you *had* to get married," Edna pointed out.

Edith sighed. "Yes."

"Did you know how I felt about him?"

"I didn't until Mother told me."

So she had known.

"I had planned to go to his brother's wedding with him, like I promised, and then stop seeing him."

"But you didn't stop."

"No, I didn't," Edith said. "He was like a drug. He was the kindest boy I'd ever met. He made me feel like I was the most beautiful creature on the planet. Honestly, I think I was addicted to all the attention."

"But on some level you must have known it would hurt me."

"I chose to ignore that feeling."

Edna snorted. Edith did not elaborate.

"But you two did stop seeing each other shortly after the wedding."

"I know. A few dates after the wedding, we—what's the term they use these days— we went all the way."

"You can just say the two of you had sex," Edna said bluntly.

Edith visibly flinched. "It just happened." She averted her gaze from Edna. "And we were ashamed because we weren't married, and we decided not to see each other anymore."

A healthcare worker rolled in a machine to take Edith's vitals. She was a robust older woman with a pretty smile, and she chattered away as she wrapped a blood pressure cuff around Edith's arm and put a pulse ox on her fingertip. She swiped a thermometer across her forehead and once the machine beeped, she smiled and said, "Everything looks good, Mrs. Bermingham."

"Thank you, Rhonda."

After Rhonda wheeled the machine out, Edna looked pointedly at her sister and asked, "Were you really pregnant?" Many times down through the years, she'd thought her sister had tricked Charley, and she wouldn't have put it past her to then conveniently "lose" the baby.

Edith was indignant. "Of course I was pregnant! I would never pull a stunt like that. When I was married to Charley, I had five miscarriages. When I married Bill, I had three more."

Edna had not known this, and she was a little taken aback by this news. The disappointment in her sister's voice was obvious, even after all this time. Edith had never struck her as the maternal type.

"I knew Charley wanted a lot of children," Edith said. "It was all he spoke about. And he was so kind, I was more than happy to have babies, especially in light of the fact that he did the decent thing and married me. If he hadn't, my life would have been ruined. Although I never thought about having kids, not like some women do, I wanted to give him children. I thought that was the one thing I could do: give him the children he wanted. Unfortunately, that didn't happen."

Charley must have been devastated, but the fact that Edith went on to have multiple pregnancies suggested to Edna that they were making it work in the bedroom.

"Then why did you divorce him?" she asked.

"Eventually it dawned on me that I wouldn't be able to give him the children he so desperately wanted. He was still young, and it wasn't fair to stay married to him."

"That was big of you," Edna said.

"Of course, his parents were livid that I wanted a divorce. As soon as I mentioned it, I was sent packing, but I was determined that we should be free of one another."

But not before all the damage was done, thought Edna. "Did you know that after you told him you wanted a divorce, Charley came to see me in Chicago?" Edna asked.

Edith shook her head. "No, I didn't. But I'm not surprised. More than once, I heard his mother tell him that he'd married the wrong sister."

It must have been awful to hear that.

"He wanted to see if his mother was right? If you were the girl for him?" Edith guessed.

"Something like that, but I said no. It was too late."

"Of course."

"And what about Bill? What happened there?" Now Edna was simply being nosy. After all, there were some gaps in their history.

"He cheated on me. I found him in bed with his secretary, which is such a cliché," Edith said with a curled lip.

To Edna it sounded like karma with all capital letters.

Edith continued. "I went through a period of depression when I realized there'd be no children and wasn't fully engaged at the time. Bill sought comfort elsewhere. But he ended up doing me a favor. If I hadn't divorced him, I would never have met Herb."

"You never sought help for all these miscarriages?" Edna asked.

"You know how it was back then. There was really no help. You either had babies or you didn't. It was never spoken of, being a childless couple."

"Things are different now," Edna said. She looked down at her ringless hands. Here they were at their age, in their late eighties, having their first adult conversation. The anger she'd held on to all those years was fading. Maybe they were too old for this sort of nonsense. Maybe Hal was right, and it was time to let go of the past and all that rage.

They both were silent, each lost in their own thoughts. Suddenly, Edna felt bone weary. She wanted to go home and take a nap. She supposed everything that needed to be said had been said.

"I should get going."

"I want to apologize to you for hurting you all those years ago. I should have apologized sooner," Edith said.

"Better late than never, I guess," Edna said with a sigh.

"That's what I really wanted to say." Edith's voice was quiet.

"Apology accepted."

Slowly, Edna pulled herself out of the chair and thought she would go in for a mini nap when she got home.

"One more thing, Edna. I have a favor to ask."

Edna frowned. She'd only just apologized and now she was looking for favors? That didn't take long.

"Please make sure I get a proper funeral."

"Edith, I see you're still dramatic. You're going home, you said so yourself."

"Please, Edna, promise me. As a favor to Mother and Dad," Edith pressed.

She couldn't refuse that. And she knew her parents would want her to make this promise.

"Of course," Edna said tightly. "If you should happen to die, I'll make sure you get a proper burial." And then she asked, "Don't you have a will?"

"I do, but I haven't left any instructions."

"Why not? I've got detailed instructions, from what I want to wear in my casket to what songs should be sung at the funeral." She had even toyed with the idea of writing her own eulogy, but Hal had talked her out of it.

"You were always more organized than me," Edith said. "It was something I thought I would have time to do."

"Do it when you get home, make up a list," Edna advised.

"I will, I promise."

"Goodbye, Edith."

"Goodbye, Edna."

Exhausted, Edna exited the room and the hospital, anxious for some fresh air. The encounter had taken a lot out of her, and she couldn't wait to get home and put her feet up. Plus, she wanted to go over what had been said. The apology surprised her; she didn't think her sister had it in her. Edna was realistic, though. At their age, she didn't think they'd become close friends. And she believed her sister knew that as well. But maybe when they met each other in public, they wouldn't have to be separated. Maybe they could be cordial to one another or at least civil. And maybe that was enough.

Chapter Thirty

Hal came in through the back door. Edna sat at her kitchen table, drinking a cup of tea. He regarded her for a moment before asking, "Well, how did it go?"

Edna nodded. "I think it went well."

"How do you feel?" he asked. Hal was all about feelings, and he was in touch with his own, which showed how progressive he was for a man his age.

"I'm not sure, really," she said truthfully. The visit with Edith, although illuminating, had left her drained. And now she was simply trying to hang on until bedtime.

"Do you feel better?" he pressed.

"I wouldn't say I feel better, but I do feel different."

The chip on her shoulder she'd been burdened with since 1957 had been knocked loose. Admittedly, she felt lighter. And casting Edith as the villain in her life story no longer worked.

"Want to go to the Annacotty Room and grab some dinner?" he asked.

"I think I would like that," Edna said. "I'm not in the mood to cook anything tonight."

"Let's go."

"But it's only three thirty," she said.

"Early bird special," he reminded her.

"Give me a minute," she said, standing up and heading off in the direction of the bathroom.

Edna crumpled up the sheet of notepaper. She was trying to put her feelings into words for her sister. But she didn't know what to say.

Dear Edith,
I appreciate your apology. I wish you peace . . .

And that was as far as she got. She pushed the pen and notepaper aside and stood, looking to do something else. She'd come back to it later. Maybe she'd have gathered her thoughts by then.

Edna headed into Coffee Girl later that week, looking for her usual, a glazed donut and a cup of coffee. The café always smelled the same: baked sugar and fresh-brewed coffee. It was heavenly. The place was crowded, and she scanned the interior looking for an unoccupied table. There were several. Satisfied, she stepped in line and noticed her sister a few people ahead of her. She'd heard that Edith had been discharged from the hospital, and that was a good thing. It was a step in the right direction.

She stepped out of line and approached her sister. She was aware that Erica, behind the till, froze, and that the entire restaurant went silent. It was as if everyone was holding their breath to see if a melee would break out between the sisters or possibly an exchange of sharp words. Edna smiled. Those days were over.

She touched her sister lightly on the arm. "Edith."

Her sister turned and gave her a smile. She was very pale, but at least she was out of the hospital.

"I heard you'd come home, and I'm glad to see you out and about."

"Thank you," Edith said softly. The person ahead of her in the line stepped away, and Edith took her place in front of the cash register.

"Enjoy your coffee," Edna said.

"Thank you, I will." As Edna turned away, Edith said, "I got your card, Edna, and I wanted to say how much I appreciated it."

"That's good."

Edna smiled at her younger sister and went back to the end of the line. The din of conversation picked up in the restaurant, and life and living resumed.

Part Three

Esther

Chapter Thirty-One

Esther received an apology request from a college-aged woman who had done something terrible to her dorm roommate, who was also her good friend. Apparently, the client had become jealous of the roommate's new boyfriend and all the time they were spending together, and schemed to break them up. And when that didn't work, she told her roommate she'd caught her boyfriend with someone else, which was untrue. It resulted in her roommate breaking up with her boyfriend and turning to her friend for support.

This was what she'd written to Esther in her email:

My friend was so miserable and depressed over the breakup that she stopped going to classes. In fact, she stopped doing anything. I wish I could go back and undo those things I said about her boyfriend. I'm caught. If I apologize, I will probably lose the friendship. And if I don't apologize, I have to live with this on my conscience.

Although in Esther's opinion the friendship had been over as soon as the girl spread malicious gossip about her friend's boyfriend, she read between the lines that the young woman was looking for unsolicited advice. Esther crafted her reply carefully:

A friendship, or for that matter any relationship, cannot exist based on lies. I agree with you that once your friend finds out what you've done, the relationship will probably be over. But you can file this under 'actions have consequences.' The good news is that you will never make this mistake again in your life.

Or Esther hoped not, at least. Relationships were such fragile things; they needed to be handled with the utmost care. She crafted an apology letter for the girl and asked her to let her know how she made out, which she did. Although her roommate appreciated both the apology and her honesty, she said it was the end of their friendship. Esther's client ended the informative email with "lesson learned."

It made Esther think about her own relationships, and how hard she'd need to work on them and on herself. But now it was time to get ready to go out for dinner with Derrick.

She took great care with her appearance as she waited for him to pick her up. They had a reservation for dinner at the Annacotty Room. She put on some mascara and eyeliner, as well as some lipstick. The great thing about summer was you had some color and didn't need to bother with foundation or blush. After she spiked her short hair with a little bit of gel, she fastened a line of small diamond studs descending toward a pair of gold hoops into the multiple piercings in her ears. Finally, she chose a violet-colored maxi dress that showed off her shoulders and arms and paired it with some dressy sandals.

"Wow! You look fantastic," Derrick said, leaning in for a kiss when he arrived. He sported a vibrant red Hawaiian-print shirt and a pair of khaki shorts that showed off his tan, muscular legs.

Pebbles stood between them, wagging her tail. The cats had disappeared. They were strange until they got to know you.

"Thanks." Esther grinned from ear to ear, pleased with the compliment.

She locked her door, and Derrick walked beside her with his hand on the small of her back, which felt oddly familiar as if they'd always walked like this. As gracefully as she could manage, she climbed up into his pickup truck, a rental. It still had that new-car smell. Her heart beat rapidly, making her feel like a teenager again.

It was a beautiful summer evening. The sky was streaked with violet, apricot, and pink. It was so pretty that Esther found herself smiling.

"I can drop you off at the door before I park," he offered as they approached the Annacotty Room.

She waved him away. "No way. I can walk. I'm not ninety."

He laughed. "Whatever the lady wants."

She pointed ahead of them. "Look, there's a free space up in front of the Quirk and the Quill."

He parked the truck, then sat back and gazed at her. "It's been nice spending time with you, Esther."

"Same here," she said. It almost felt like old times.

They walked down Main Street toward the front entrance of the restaurant. Derrick held the door for her and as they entered, Lou and his sister, Carol, were exiting. Esther froze. Lou looked at her and then swung his gaze over to Derrick and seemed to draw his own conclusions.

Carol smiled and approached Esther, throwing her arms around her. "Esther, it's wonderful to see you." Her glance slid sideways to Derrick, but her expression was unreadable.

"How are you, Carol?"

"I'm well. Dragged my brother out of the house for some dinner," she said.

"Hello, Es," Lou said.

"Hello, Lou," she said softly. Why did she feel embarrassed about being seen out with Derrick? What was that all about? She felt as if she were eight and had been caught playing with her mother's lipstick and nail polish.

Esther had always liked Lou's sister. She was friendly and liked a good laugh. She was pretty, with caramel-colored hair and blonde highlights and dark brown eyes. She was dressed in a white linen outfit, and a diamond tennis bracelet sparkled on her wrist.

They all stood there for a long, awkward moment. Finally, Derrick thrust his hand toward Lou. "Derrick Radich."

"Lou Gunderman," he replied, shaking Derrick's hand with what appeared to be reluctance. "This is my sister, Carol Kelley."

Before they had to endure any more awkward silences, Esther took a deep breath and said to Derrick, "We better go in. We have a reservation and I'm starving."

"It was nice to see you again," Lou said as if they'd been mere acquaintances. That stung a bit. He followed his sister out of the restaurant.

"Old flame?" Derrick asked.

Esther's skin prickled. "Something like that." She wasn't going to get into it with Derrick. Running into Lou had set her off balance, leaving her with a hollow feeling in her stomach. Why did she feel so awful about being "caught" with Derrick? It wasn't like she was cheating on Lou. She and Derrick were just friends. Why did her heart ache? She hadn't missed the pained expression on Lou's face. And as someone who was all too familiar with heartbreak, she'd felt sorry for him.

They were seated at a table in a corner of the back room, and their server handed them their menus. Esther knew the menu by heart and asked to hear what the specials of the day were. She studied the wine list but couldn't focus because she was still thinking about Lou. She realized Derrick was talking to her.

"I'm sorry, did you say something?" she said.

With a smile, he reached across the table and took hold of her hands. "I said you look beautiful tonight."

She could feel her face redden, and she was determined to put Lou out of her mind. She'd been looking forward to this evening and she didn't want to ruin it by feeling guilty.

Derrick gave her hands a gentle squeeze. "You have no idea how much I've been looking forward to tonight."

The server reappeared to take their orders. "Now, what will we have to drink?" he asked.

"Let's get a bottle of wine," Esther said. They could always leave Derrick's truck parked here and walk home later if need be.

"That's a great idea," Derrick replied.

With a wink, she said, "I thought so too."

They shared an appetizer of coconut jumbo shrimp with a mango sauce. They sipped wine and spoke easily. It amazed her that they seemed to have picked up where they left off, as if they'd never been apart. She encouraged him to take the last piece of shrimp. When he finished, he sipped his wine and said softly, "I want to apologize for how things ended between us."

"It was a long time ago."

"I hope there's no statute of limitations on apologies," he said.

She shook her head. "None at all."

"I've thought about you a lot over the years."

Esther lifted an eyebrow.

"Actually, I've given it a lot of thought," he said with a laugh. "I wish I had met you later, when I was more mature, more settled. We were so young back then. We weren't ready to settle down."

She'd been ready; she'd been looking forward to it. And a year after he dumped her, he'd married someone else. But she chose not to mention these things. Why ruin a perfectly good apology.

Derrick took a gulp of his wine. "Well, anyway, I wanted to say I'm sorry."

She couldn't help but be impressed. It took a lot of courage and integrity to say you were sorry. Even after all this time.

"Thank you," she said.

Derrick poured more wine into their glasses.

The server appeared and cleared their appetizer dishes, informing them that their dinners would be out shortly.

When he left, Derrick continued. "When I ran into you here in Lavender Bay, I was surprised to realize that not only was I happy to see you, but there were still some feelings there."

"Really?"

"Why does that surprise you?" he asked, grinning.

"I don't know. You were the one who broke it off, I figured you never gave me a second thought."

"Just because I broke it off between us doesn't mean I didn't love you. More than anything, I regret hurting you," Derrick said quietly. He swirled his wine glass in his hand.

Esther was at a loss for words. At the time, she had been devastated, of that there was no doubt. To hear him acknowledge that pain was satisfying. She could practically feel the wound closing up.

"Looking back on things, I was a fool to let you go," he said.

Funny, she'd always hoped he regretted dumping her, but her thoughts were different now. "That's the thing, though, isn't it, Derrick? We can all look back and wish we'd done something differently, but you're questioning that decision based on the person you are now, not the person you were then."

Derrick looked at her blankly and then burst out laughing. "Esther, that's quite philosophical."

She'd had a lot of time to think about things. "Now what?" she asked.

He smiled and shook his head. He set his wine glass down and picked up his fork and fiddled with it. "I'm here for a few more weeks. Why don't we continue to see one another."

More than anything, Esther needed clarity. "What are you looking for? Casual dating? A relationship?" She wouldn't take the chance of being blindsided again.

He chuckled. "You get right to the point."

"It's important for me to know where I stand."

"I can assure you that right now, you're standing in a good place. I would like to explore things between us."

Esther was shocked. She hadn't expected a conversation like this with him. They hadn't seen each other in so long.

With great hesitation, if only to temper any excitement, she said quietly, "Me too." She would be careful here. It was funny how as you aged, you became more practical and sensible. She'd only broken up with Lou a few months ago, and she certainly hadn't been looking for anything serious. She wasn't twenty. There would be no rushing headlong into a new relationship here.

"That's great," he said.

She was compelled to add a disclaimer. "But let's keep things easy and open-ended."

"Agreed."

The server appeared with their dinners. Esther smiled down at the filet on her plate, thinking it was going to be a beautiful evening.

Chapter Thirty-Two

Esther was looking forward to the next two weeks. It was the start of her inaugural summer bowling camp for kids. She was on vacation from her IT job, and she put the apology writing aside for the time being.

Sophie, Margret, and Becky had offered to assist during the two weeks of bowling camp. She gladly accepted. Twenty-five children needed a lot of supervision, and the girls were a big help. Included in the group of twenty-five were her nephews Patrick and Jason, and Rose's boy, Connor.

Esther didn't know who was more excited about bowling camp: herself or the kids that had signed up. The bowling alley, usually quiet on weekday mornings, was now punctuated with the shouts and laughter of the kids.

She gathered everyone around her to go over the rules of behavior while they were at the lanes. The child who needed to hear it most, Jimmy Melvin, nephew of Debbie, was talking nonstop to a kid in the back row.

"Jimmy? Jimmy?" Esther said, a little louder the second time. He looked at her, his expression blank. "I need you and everyone to pay attention here."

"Okay," he grumbled.

She sorted the kids into two groups: younger and older. She left the girls in charge of the younger kids as she felt she needed to keep an eye on eleven-year-old Jimmy, who was in with the older group.

The first task was to make sure each kid had a properly fitted ball. The girls helped her with this, and it didn't take too long. Then she moved onto instruction and skill building, thinking they'd concentrate on one skill at the start of each morning. Esther ran between the two groups, giving them each one lesson to learn, dropping such gems as "Remember your swing is your thing," and "Stay in your lane." As camp progressed, she'd teach them about the correct body posture and how to throw their balls accurately.

The second and third hours were where the actual game playing began. She taught the kids how to use the scoreboard and assigned scorekeepers in pairs so they could help one another.

She stood at the back of the lane as the older group started to bowl an actual game. One kid in particular was having difficulty—he certainly seemed to have mastered the gutter ball angle. Esther approached him and gave him some pointers, and when he threw the ball, he knocked down one pin.

Progress.

But behind her, someone yelled, "Ya loser!"

She closed her eyes and sighed. Jimmy. She turned around and said, "Jimmy, that is not helpful."

On his follow-up turn, the kid knocked down two pins. Jimmy made another smart comment.

"All right, who's next?" she asked, and a fourteen-year-old girl named Amy stepped up and retrieved her bowling ball from the ball return rack.

"You okay, Amy?" Esther asked.

The girl nodded.

Esther stepped off the lane and approached Jimmy, who was fooling heavily with another kid on the bench. "Jimmy, come here, please." She steered him away from the group, out of earshot.

"There's no need to shout insults at the other players," she said to him.

Jimmy wore a confused expression. "Why not?"

"Calling people losers is not nice."

He shrugged. "It's just a joke."

"Would you like to be treated like that?" she asked, searching his face to see if she was getting through to him at all. It was doubtful. "How would you like it if someone called you a loser?"

"But that won't happen, because I'm a good bowler," he said proudly.

That much was true. "Let's say you threw a gutter ball," she said.

"But I wouldn't."

Esther closed her eyes for a moment and said a quick prayer for patience. "Humor me and say you did."

He nodded but remained unconvinced.

"How would you feel if someone started calling you names?"

"I'd clobber them!" he said loudly.

"Jimmy, haven't you ever heard of the golden rule?" she asked.

He nodded enthusiastically. Esther thought, *Finally, I'm making some headway.*

Jimmy spoke. "Dad loves the golden rule!"

Somehow this surprised her, but she was encouraged. All was not lost with the Melvin family.

"Over at Golden Pizza," Jimmy said, "the golden rule is if you buy one large pepperoni pizza, you get the second one half off!"

Esther's mouth hung open but no words came out.

As Jimmy returned to his lane, Esther leaned into Becky, who'd overheard the exchange and was giggling. "We've got to keep an eye on him."

At noon, when all the kids had been picked up by their parents, Esther was a happy kind of exhausted.

She made sure they were all gone before packing up her own gear. Sophie, Margret, and Becky headed off to the beach with money Esther had given them for Scoopalicious. On her way out, she waved goodbye to Lenny and told him she'd see him the following day.

There was dinner at Gail's later that evening. It would be a full house with Rose and her family, but Esther didn't mind that at all, thinking they could serve as a buffer between her and Suzanne.

Esther was the last to arrive. Suzanne, Ray, and the kids were already there. When she stepped outside to the backyard, there was a strong smell of barbecue from the grill, and her mouth watered. She hadn't invited Derrick to join her, thinking her family wasn't ready to see him yet. She'd told him she'd meet him later at the bowling alley.

Ray stood at the grill, barbecue tools in hand.

"Smells good, Ray," Esther said.

He smiled. "Marinated chicken, my secret recipe." And he returned his attention to the grill.

"Where are the girls?" Esther asked.

"They're still at the beach," Rose replied.

Esther was happy to hear that Becky was spending time with her nieces. Hopefully the time up here would take her mind off her problems back home. At least for a while.

"Mom, I've got the potato salad and the macaroni salad," Esther said. "Do you want me to put them in the fridge?"

"No, put them on the table with the rest of the stuff. I don't think it will be long before we eat." Gail cast her attention to Ray. "Ray, how long before the chicken is done?"

"I'd say five minutes, Gail." He opened the grill and turned over the chicken with the tongs, narrowing his eyes as a large plume of smoke drifted up from the grill. The meat sizzled on the rack.

Esther set the two bowls of salad on the picnic table, leaving the cling wrap on them until they were ready to eat. The table was stocked with paper plates, a silverware caddy, and a tossed salad and a fruit salad under mesh domes to keep the bees and flies away. There were condiments and pitchers of iced tea and lemonade. Beneath the table was a cooler full of cans of soda on ice.

The lawn chairs were placed in a semi-circle. Gail, Suzanne, Lydia, and Rose sat around, gabbing. Beneath Gail's lawn chair, Rufus was stretched out, snoring and farting.

Patrick and Jason sat with Connor at the picnic table, showing him something on their phones.

Esther took the empty chair next to Rose.

"How's everything going?" she asked her cousin.

"Great, we've been on the go since we got here."

"I'm going to need a vacation when I get home," Aunt Lydia said.

"Hey, thanks for letting Connor join the bowling camp," Rose said. "He said it was a lot of fun."

"Good."

"It's a shame we have to leave before the camp ends. We'll know for next time."

"Do you think you'll come back soon?" Suzanne asked.

"Definitely. We're having too much fun not to."

"Provided Gail doesn't mind us staying with her," Lydia said softly.

"Not at all!" Gail said. "The company has been good for me. I have all these rooms and no one to use them. You're always welcome."

"How's Becky getting on?" Esther asked Rose.

"Great," Rose said enthusiastically. "We've hardly seen her. She spends all her time with Sophie and Margret. They've been so good to her."

"I'm glad to hear that."

"Me too. What a relief." Rose looked off into the distance and spoke quietly. "It's nice to see her so animated again. I've missed that."

"Chicken's ready!" Ray announced.

As they all sat at the picnic table eating their grilled chicken with salad, Esther said, "You did a great job with the chicken, Ray."

Ray looked as if he could hardly believe his sister-in-law had singled him out to speak to him. It made Esther feel like a real tool. But she'd only spoken the truth. The grilled chicken was delicious.

"Thanks, Esther," he said.

She was aware of Suzanne's eyes on her. But Esther was engaged with Aunt Lydia in conversation about the different ways they made their potato salad. Aunt Lydia added a little vinegar to hers and used only Miracle Whip. Esther microwaved her potatoes because she couldn't stand to wait on potatoes boiling in a pot. The late afternoon heat settled around them and once again, she thought, like she did every day, about how much she loved summer and everything that went along with it.

Suzanne and Ray left early with the boys because they had a baseball game. They invited Connor to go with them and initially he was hesitant, but when Aunt Lydia said she'd go along too, he readily agreed, all smiles.

Rose helped Esther with the cleanup. As they carried the leftovers into the house, Rose asked, "Is everything all right between you and Suzanne?" When Esther didn't say anything, Rose added, "I've noticed you two hardly speak to one another."

Esther sighed, opening a cupboard door and searching for tin foil. "Sister stuff, that's all. It'll blow over." But it had been going on for a while, and now she wasn't so sure.

"I'd give anything to have a sister."

Esther snorted. "You're welcome to mine." She found the tin foil and ripped off a sheet to cover one of the bowls of salad. Rose waited for further explanation, and Esther felt compelled to say something, but she kept silent. She wasn't about to tell her it was because she didn't like Ray.

As Rose filled the sink with water and a squirt of dish soap, she said, "Growing up as an only child, I was lonely most of the time, especially after we moved to Florida. It was awful."

"I didn't know that," Esther said. It was hard to imagine someone as beautiful as Rose being lonely or sad.

Rose nodded and set the grill racks in the soapy water.

"You don't need to do that, Rose, I can do those," Esther said.

"I don't mind. It's the least I can do. Your mother has been so wonderful to us."

"She loves having you here, that much is true."

Esther began to load the dishwasher. "What are your plans for the night?"

Rose shrugged, taking a steel wool pad to the grill racks. "With both kids gone, I plan on getting comfortable in the backyard with my book, which I haven't been able to read in over a week."

"I'm going bowling, you're welcome to join us," Esther offered.

Rose paused, the steel wool poised in her hand. "I appreciate that. But I'll give it a pass. We've been out every day since I've been here, and I'm actually looking forward to doing nothing tonight."

"I get that. Another time."

"Definitely. Because I have nothing against bowling." Rose winked at her cousin.

Esther laughed. "Yes, I love bowling."

"So I've heard!"

Chapter Thirty-Three

Derrick was waiting for Esther at the bowling alley. Lakeside Bowling Lanes was all but empty. Esther loved the place in all weather and in all seasons. But there was something special about the summer, when she often felt like she had the whole place to herself. Derrick broke into a grin when she arrived, and he leaned in and kissed her on the cheek. He smelled of a spicy cologne, which she decided was nice.

Lenny Bastich was on duty and assigned Esther to her favorite lane, lucky lane six. The old man eyed Derrick with a side glance. Derrick took off his deck shoes and traded them in for a pair of bowling shoes, and Lenny put them in a small wooden cubby and gave him a claim ticket.

Esther carried her bag over to the lane while Derrick went in search of a ball. The air conditioning was going full blast, and Esther tugged on a light cardigan, glad she'd brought it along.

She set down her bag, took a seat on the bench, and swapped out her sandals for a pair of ankle socks and her bowling shoes. At the next lane, Derrick was slipping his fingers into different bowling balls and lifting them up, testing their weight. Finally, after the seventh or eighth ball, he found one that seemed a good fit and carried it over and set it in the ball rack next to Esther's.

Esther got comfortable at the lane table and set up the automatic scorer, which showed a visual overhead. Usually, she liked to keep score on paper, the old-fashioned way, but she opted for the more convenient way today.

"I haven't bowled since high school," Derrick said, sliding onto the bench seat next to her.

"Really? You loved bowling when we were in school," she said. It was how she'd met him. At bowling club.

He grinned, laughing. "I only joined to meet you. I had no interest in the game."

"I did not know that." Esther was surprised.

"It's true. I'd seen you around school and since I was a year ahead of you, there was no way we were going to share a class together."

It had been a long time since Esther had been the subject of unbridled flattery.

"You were in the drama club," he went on, "and what a relief it was when you left that and joined the bowling club. As much as I liked you, I couldn't see myself joining an acting troupe. So it was a good day for me when you quit drama."

It had been a good day for Esther, too, because it had been her introduction to the sport of bowling. That sign-up turned into one of the most pleasurable pastimes of her life.

"Would you like to go first?" she asked with a nod toward the lane.

"Ladies first. I insist," he replied.

"All right then."

Esther went first and Derrick followed. He was a little rusty to begin with but then improved. Apparently his natural athletic ability was still intact. He'd played multiple sports in high school. She wondered if he still did. It made her realize how much she didn't know about him or what he had been doing in the last twenty-five years.

When she threw her third strike in a row, he called out from his seat at the lane table, "You're on fire."

"That's a turkey."

"What do you mean?" he protested. "Three strikes in a row? That's great!"

She laughed. "No, that's what it's called. Don't you remember? Three strikes in a row is called a turkey."

"Oh. I'm not up to date on all the terminology."

Esther smiled. "It's all right, because I am."

"You really like this bowling thing, don't you?" he asked.

She was about to say it was her life but bit her tongue, thinking it might look kind of pathetic. "We all have hobbies."

"We do. I prefer to be outside myself. You don't mind being cooped up in here on a hot summer day?"

"I'd be here if there was a Category 5 hurricane going on outside," she replied.

After two games, she said, "Are you up for a third?" She was hopeful.

He shook his head. "I'm good for another twenty-five years."

She chuckled, trying to cover her disappointment. "All right."

When they went outside, they landed right in the twilight hour. The sky was a grayish blue, and the streetlights were on. Up the street, a group of kids loitered beneath a streetlight. In the opposite direction, an elderly couple walked along enjoying ice cream cones.

Derrick glanced across the street at Dog Days Bar. "Look, it's karaoke night over there. Let's do it."

"Karaoke?" Esther said. She'd rather have a root canal without anesthetic.

"Come on, it'll be fun."

For Esther it sounded anything but. But before she could protest any further, he relieved her of her bowling ball case and hauled it across the street to the bar. She paused. Karaoke wasn't her thing. It was down to one thing and one thing only: she was a terrible singer.

Despite all this, she followed him over to the bar. As soon as he opened the door, noise spilled out. She hadn't even stepped into the place and she was already being treated to someone singing poorly. Inside, a woman Esther's age was up on the stage butchering Patsy Cline's "Walkin' After Midnight."

Esther couldn't remember the last time she'd been into Dog Days. Probably in her twenties. It still smelled the same: of Pine Sol and stale beer. Derrick was already leaning against the bar, trying to get the bartender's attention. He looked over his shoulder at Esther. "What do you want to drink?"

"Pepsi's fine," she said. She'd driven, so no alcohol for her. She looked down at her precious bowling case. Derrick had set it on the floor, which she was pretty sure was tacky with spilled drinks.

Once Derrick had procured their drinks, he spotted a table and led Esther over to it. He didn't sit down, though, instead saying to her, "I'll go put our names on the list for karaoke."

Her eyebrows lifted so high they were practically at her hairline. "You go ahead. I can't sing."

"Neither can I. Come on, I can't go up there by myself."

Before she could protest further, he disappeared, heading toward the back of the bar where the karaoke action was taking place.

When he returned he was all smiles. "There's only five people ahead of us." He followed that up with, "We won't have to wait long," as Esther was thinking, *We have to wait that long?*

By the time they were called up for their turn, Esther had accepted her fate. But from the slightly elevated impromptu stage, she looked out at the crowd present, realizing she recognized many people from town and thus, they her. Her mouth went dry and her hands, clammy. Derrick hadn't noticed; he was too busy trying to select a song. The first three he picked, Esther shook her head, telling him, "I don't even know those songs." He was determined to sing a country song and finally they agreed to try "Take Me Home, Country Roads" as it was one of the few country and western songs she knew.

"Will we do different parts?" Derrick asked.

"Huh? What?"

"I'll sing one stanza, and you sing the next," he suggested brightly.

Oh no, he's a karaoke enthusiast, she thought. "If it's all the same to you, I prefer to sing them together." She'd need his voice to mask her own.

The music started playing, a microphone was shoved in her hand, and the lyrics started rolling across the screen. She and Derrick leaned in together to sing. Halfway through, she thought, *I didn't know this song was this looong.* She could have sworn she saw a couple people in the crowd wince as they sang. When they were finished, there was lukewarm but polite applause. As they made their way over to the bar, she made sure her bowling ball was still where she'd left it. The first thought that popped into her head was *Thank God I work from home, because I'll never be able to leave it again.*

"That was fun, wasn't it?" Derrick asked, ordering another beer and Pepsi from the bartender.

Was it?

He slid a twenty-dollar bill across the bar, waited for his change, tipped the bartender, who acknowledged it with a nod, and handed Esther her Pepsi. "You can pick the next song." He tipped the beer bottle back and took a long gulp.

"I think one is enough for me," Esther said.

"Aw, come on." He leaned into her and nudged her shoulder with his own. "Esther, you've got to admit it was fun."

"I plead the fifth," she said, and she set her glass down on the bar.

Derrick burst out laughing. "Still the same old Esther."

"Is that good or bad?"

"Oh, it's good," he said with a quick nod.

Before she could think of something to say that would get him off the topic of karaoke, he said, "I'll go put our names back on the list."

"Okay," she said weakly.

They sang one more song. This time, she did choose: "It's Raining Men," a song she was sure the crowd would join in on. And sure enough, the women in the crowd sang along, raising the volume on their voices, practically lifting the roof off the bar. All of this did not make the karaoke any more fun for Esther, but at least she wasn't alone in her misery. The sisterhood had rescued her.

Later as they walked out of Dog Days, Derrick said, "They have karaoke every Thursday night if you're interested. We might be able to go a few more times before I head back to Florida."

Esther winced. "Oh, I'm sorry, but I can't. That's league night for me." Now, leagues didn't start until September, but Derrick didn't need to know that. If karaoke night was on Thursdays, then Esther was going to be otherwise occupied.

Chapter Thirty-Four

Everyone gathered at Suzanne's house for dinner the night before Rose and her family were due to leave. Suzanne and Ray had moved into a new build in a subdivision of new homes. It was perfect for the kids as it was a neighborhood of young families.

Esther had texted Suzanne and asked if she could bring anything, and had received a response of *Dessert would be great*. She walked up the wide two-car driveway, carrying two thirteen by nine pans stacked on top of each other. One held a Watergate cake and the other a two-layer cheesecake. Both recipes were from Grammy and still made regular appearances at family gatherings. Watergate cake was always Esther's choice for her birthday, and she'd eat no other cheesecake but this one, made with sour cream and cream cheese.

Sophie and Margret sat on the front lawn with Becky. They were huddled together, laughing and giggling about something. That warmed Esther's heart.

"Hey, girls," she called out.

In unison, they all replied, "Hi, Aunt Esther." This caused them to break into giggles again. Esther shook her head but was laughing as she landed on the porch. Realizing she didn't have a free hand, she peered through the screen door. She saw no one but heard voices at the back of the house.

"Knock, knock, anyone home?" she called.

Ray soon appeared and opened the screen door. "Here, let me take that from you."

She handed off the desserts to her brother-in-law, thanked him, and followed him into the house, closing the door behind her.

Rose and Aunt Lydia were already in the kitchen, along with Gail and Suzanne. Gail sat with Aunt Lydia at the table, ready to eat.

Rose stood against the counter, arms folded across her chest as she talked to Suzanne, who stood at the stove stirring beef and broccoli around in a wok. She looked over her shoulder at Esther. "You made it."

Unsure if it was a barbed comment or not, Esther took the high road and said, "I never pass up a dinner invitation."

Ray had set the desserts down on the counter, and Esther took the cheesecake and made room for it in the refrigerator. To Rose, she said, "Are you all ready to leave?"

Rose tilted her head in one direction and then the other. "Not really." Then, laughing, she added, "I'll probably be running around later like a chicken with my head cut off, throwing everything into our suitcases."

"Boy, the two weeks went by fast," Suzanne said. She gave the rice a stir and scooped it all out of the pot, transferring it to a bowl and fluffing it up with a fork.

"Ugh, it sure did. The only thing waiting for me at home is work," Rose said with a roll of her eyes. They turned their heads toward the sound of raucous laughter from the front yard. Rose smiled. "I can't thank you enough. This has been so good for Becky. Sophie and Margret have been so kind to her."

"The three girls have had a great time, haven't they," Suzanne said.

"I'm glad to hear that," Esther said.

Ray interrupted and asked, "Suze, how long before dinner?"

"I'm putting it on the table right now."

He went to the front door and called in the girls. Then he went to the back door and announced to the boys that dinner was ready. He then took a seat at the table, waiting. Esther thought her brother-in-law could have carried some things over to the table to help Suzanne, but she reminded herself that it wasn't her place to interfere. Or, for that matter, even to have an opinion about it.

Esther took the large pasta bowl that held the rice over to the table, and Suzanne carried the wok full of beef and broccoli. Both were laid on hot pads next to the bowl of tossed salad and bottle of soy sauce.

Suzanne walked around the table and filled the water glasses. Esther took a seat between Patrick and Jason. Everyone passed their plates to Suzanne, who ladled generous portions of rice and beef and broccoli onto each plate.

"Suze, bring over the salt, will you?" Ray asked.

Esther said nothing. Kept her head down and her eyes on her plate. *It's none of your business*, she reminded herself.

As they ate, the conversation was general.

"You're probably looking forward to going home, Connor," Ray said, shoveling his dinner into his mouth. To no one in particular, he said, "You should see this kid with a bat."

Connor shrugged. "I'd like to stay here."

"I definitely want to stay here," Becky said. "I don't want to go home." Her expression turned sullen, and the table went quiet.

Esther took the plunge. "Maybe you could stay a little while longer." She knew she shouldn't interfere, but she couldn't help herself.

"That wouldn't be possible," Rose said.

Becky's face had brightened considerably with Esther's suggestion that she stay. She turned to her mother and said, "Can I? Can I?"

"No, you—"

Sophie and Margret chimed in. "Aw, come on, Cousin Rose, let her stay. We're having so much fun."

Rose shook her head. "I can't impose on Aunt Gail's hospitality any longer."

Gail shrugged her shoulders. "It's not a problem. I don't mind at all. It's nice having someone in the house."

"She can stay here with us," Suzanne offered.

Since it had been Esther's idea, she said, "Becky, why don't you stay with me?" Gail was gone all day, six days a week at her shop, and Suzanne's house was already full with four kids. It was the perfect solution; Esther worked from home, and she had more energy for a teenager than her mother.

Becky's eyes were bright. "Can I?"

"Sure, why not?"

"Oh, I don't know." Rose sounded unconvinced.

"Let her stay, she's having so much fun," Aunt Lydia piped in. "There's only a few more weeks left of summer."

Rose looked to her mother as if seeking reassurance, and her mother gave her a slight nod. She turned to Esther. "I don't want to impose . . ."

"You're not imposing at all. I still have another week's vacation for the bowling camp," Esther told her.

"Only if you're sure."

"I'm more than sure, I'm positive," Esther said.

"How will she get back to Florida?" Rose asked.

"I'll fly her back down," Esther said.

"That's too much trouble."

"Not at all. We'll figure it out as we go," Gail said.

A happy air settled over the table as they finished their dinner. Connor looked at his mother. "Can I stay too?" he asked.

"No, sweetie. Not this time."

"Aw."

"I think it's time for dessert," Suzanne said, and she stood to get the cakes.

Esther stood, gathered dessert plates and forks, and carried them to the table.

As Suzanne cut up the cakes, she said, "Who wants what? Or you can do what I do and have a slice of each."

"Both for me, Suze," Ray said. She served him, and with plate in hand, he walked away to the family room and turned on the big-screen television.

"You'd never know you had four kids," Rose said to Suzanne, eyeing her plate with two desserts on it.

"But I know," Suzanne joked. "And so does my body."

The excitement in the girls' voices was palpable now that Becky was staying longer in Lavender Bay. Once all the kids finished their desserts, they ran outside, leaving the women alone at the table. The conversation turned to raising kids, with Suzanne and Rose comparing notes. Gail and Lydia added their own versions of what it was like back in the day when they were raising children.

Whenever a conversation revolved around kids, Esther always felt left out. There was nothing for her to say or even add. She had a general idea of what it took to raise them but having never done it, she was no authority. It was one of the few subjects where she kept her mouth shut.

"We forgot the wine," Gail said. "I brought a Beaujolais over."

"I'll get it, Mom," Esther said.

"Bring some wine glasses over too, Esther," Suzanne said.

Although Suzanne had been speaking to her in civil, polite terms all evening, Esther missed their usual banter. It made her kind of sad.

"Are you anxious to go home?" Gail asked Lydia.

Esther poured the wine and handed out the glasses.

"I am, actually. Although I loved seeing everyone, I've got my routine."

"Are you busy?"

"Busy?" Rose repeated with a snort. "She's never home!"

All eyes were on Lydia.

"I belong to a lot of groups and clubs," Lydia told them. "To stay active."

"That's the secret to old age," Gail said.

"Is it?" Suzanne asked.

"You sit down, you die," Gail said with authority.

Esther laughed into her wine glass. "That's cheery, Mom."

"It's true, though. It's important to keep moving," Lydia said.

"Then you'll probably live forever, Mom," Rose said with a laugh.

"Are you seeing anyone, Rose?" Gail asked, getting right to the point.

It was the kind of personal question that made Esther cringe, although she was actually surprised her mother had left it this long. If she were sitting next to her, she would have elbowed her

"Nothing serious," Rose replied. Her tone suggested dissatisfaction. But she smiled brightly and said, "What about you, Aunt Gail? Are you romantically involved?"

Gail snorted so hard she almost spit out her wine, making Esther and Suzanne laugh.

"Goodness, no. When Hugh died, that was it for me."

"Gosh, Aunt Gail, you were so young then."

"I wasn't even fifty," Gail said. Her expression turned wistful. "Hugh was the best. No man would ever be able to hold a candle to him."

"Don't you ever get lonely?" Rose asked.

Gail didn't even have to think about it. "Not on your life. Between the shop, the grands, and my sister, I keep pretty busy. Come on, girls, let's have a toast."

The four of them lifted up their wine glasses and Gail said, "To lovers, old and new, may they bring us happiness."

"Hear, hear." Suzanne smiled, clinking her glass against her mother's.

Rose looked at Esther and Suzanne and added, "And to sisters and friends!"

Chapter Thirty-Five

With Becky staying with her for a couple more weeks, Esther rearranged her workspace in her home. She could hardly conduct business from her kitchen table if Becky was sitting around on the couch. Luckily, she had a three-bedroom home. She'd put her guest in the spare room with the pullout couch and decided to make the smallest of the three bedrooms into a home office. She had been meaning to do this for a while: create a designated workspace to keep her work life separated from her home life, which was hard to do when you worked from home. But now, here was her chance. The third room was a mess. It was a room where she stored and dumped all things to be dealt with later, but later never came around. No time like the present, she thought.

She tackled the spare bedroom with determination. She began clearing it out, removing anything she hadn't used or looked at in the past year and piling it on the living room sofa. She picked up and examined a clay cooking pot, wondering what kitchen party she'd bought that at. It was still in its original box, never having been used. After a couple of hours, the pile had grown considerably. Now that the room was cleared out, she realized she'd have to get a small desk and chair. But she knew if she stopped what she was doing to go online to order something, she'd fall down the rabbit hole of the internet and not finish what she'd started. So she kept moving. She filled a bucket with warm water and Murphy Oil Soap, washing down the baseboards, the windowsills, and the closet doors. As she was pulling out the vacuum, her doorbell rang.

Pebbles came running in from the kitchen, jumping and barking.

"Calm down," she said.

Esther had just reached the door when the bell rang a second time. She was surprised to see Edna Knickerbocker standing on her front step.

"Mrs. Knickerbocker! What brings you here?"

"Hello, Esther, may I come in?" Mrs. Knickerbocker held her handbag and her sunglasses in one hand. She wore a simple T-shirt with small cornflowers on it and a tiny bow in the center of the neckline. Her pants were tan and of a gauzy material.

"Of course." Esther held the door open, and Mrs. Knickerbocker stepped in and looked around.

"You've got a nice place here, Esther," she said.

Pebbles jumped around in front of her, and Edna regarded her with a frown. "Does she bite?"

Esther shook her head. "No. She likes company, though."

Tentatively, Mrs. Knickerbocker reached down and tapped the dog on the top of her head. Esther knew the older woman had no pets.

"Did you ever have a dog?" Esther asked. To Pebbles, she said, "Go lay down, now." The dog gave her a judgy look and toddled over to her bed, hopped up on it, and settled down with a groan of protest.

Edna shook her head. "No. I never wanted to be tied down." She looked through the sliding glass door to the backyard and her eyes widened. "I didn't know you had a pool."

"Would you like to go sit outside?" Esther asked. Her curiosity was growing by the minute as to why the older woman had stopped by. She was surprised she even knew where she lived.

"No, thank you, dear. I won't take up too much of your time."

"Have a seat."

Esther moved a few piles from the sofa so Mrs. Knickerbocker could sit down. "Apologies, I'm cleaning out my spare room."

"No problem."

Esther sat in the occasional chair and crossed her legs. "I'm sorry, Mrs. Knickerbocker, would you like something to drink?"

Edna shook her head. "No thank you. I'll get to the point. I'm coming from Nadine's home."

"My cousin? From the inn?"

"Yes. I'm looking for advice. You know about my relationship with my sister, Edith. The whole town knows."

"I do," Esther said with a nod.

"How do you maintain your relationship with your sister?" Edna asked.

"As it happens, Suzanne and I are currently struggling with a few issues at the moment."

Edna lifted an eyebrow. "Will you be able to resolve it?"

"I'm hopeful." Although at the back of Esther's mind, a little voice was saying that she'd better fix it soon as the tension between them had been going on for most of the summer.

"How do you get over the hump?"

"Very carefully. Whatever it is that we argue about"—Esther saw no need to divulge the reason for their current impasse—"we both know that we're not going to let it come between us."

"You forgive and forget?"

"We really have no choice."

"Golly, Edith and I must have been absent from school the day they were teaching that lesson."

Esther laughed.

"I see how close you and Suzanne are," Edna said, "and I see how close the Cook sisters are. And it looks like it would be hard to maintain."

"Not really. Suzanne is not only my sister but my best friend. I tell her everything. There are no secrets between us." Saying all this made her realize how much she missed her sister's company.

"Really?" Edna seemed genuinely surprised by this.

Esther nodded. "My mother has always said Suzanne would be the person I would know the longest in my life, especially the older I got. And that's true. We share common memories and a common upbringing, and that bonds us."

"But surely you must have fought down through the years? Disagreed?" Edna asked.

Esther laughed. "We fought like cats and dogs, especially when we were young."

"Interesting. Nadine said the same thing."

"I think it's unavoidable with sisters. You're going to fight. End of."

"But how do you move on?"

"You have to forgive and forget," Esther repeated.

"That easy?" Edna seemed unconvinced.

"It's that easy and it's that hard."

Edna contemplated this.

"Of course, Mrs. Knickerbocker, you and Mrs. B have done plenty of fighting over the years, maybe now you can do the easy part."

Edna cackled. "That is true, isn't it?" The elderly woman stood. "I won't take up any more of your time. I appreciate you seeing me on such short notice."

Esther almost burst out laughing. There'd been no notice. "Not a problem, Mrs. Knickerbocker."

Edna looked as if she had more to say. "I thought Edith and I were unique in all the fighting and not getting along."

Esther smiled. "Not at all. This is how it is with most sisters."

With a great sigh, Edna said, "I might have missed the boat somewhere along the way."

Esther was about to say something when Edna's eyes landed on the pile of things to be discarded. "Is that a clay pot?" Edna asked.

"It is. I'm doing a clear-out."

Boldly, Edna stepped over to the pile and picked up the box holding the clay pot. "I used to have one of these a long time ago. They're fantastic."

"Take that one. It's brand new. I've never used it," Esther said.

"Are you sure?" Mrs. Knickerbocker asked.

Gesturing toward the pile, Esther told her, "That's all headed for the garbage."

"You're throwing all this stuff away?"

"I am." Noting the older woman's interest, Esther told her, "You're welcome to any or all of it."

In the end, Esther helped Mrs. Knickerbocker carry everything out of the house she was interested in. Among the things she'd helped herself to were a lamp, a pair of old drapes, a carry-on suitcase that had seen better days, and a set of bedsheets still in the package that had been the wrong size for Esther's bed.

Chapter Thirty-Six

Esther made an unplanned trip to the grocery store. Now that she had a houseguest, she had to make sure there was enough to eat. She'd asked what Becky usually ate for breakfast and lunch, and the girl was hesitant until Esther told her it was better she speak up. That way, she could buy what Becky liked rather than her having to eat what Esther chose for her. Currently, Becky was over at Suzanne's for dinner. Her sister had said she'd drop her off later. Esther had given Becky a key in case she wasn't home.

On the way home from the grocery store, she swung by Maureen's to see if she was around. As she parked in front of the house, Maureen was walking down her driveway, popping earbuds into her ears. When she spotted Esther, she waved, removed her earbuds, and waited for her on the apron of the driveway.

"Hey there, what brings you around?" Maureen asked.

"Just looking for a chat."

"Sure, come on. Do you mind walking with me?"

"Not at all," Esther said.

"We've been out to dinner a lot, and I've been eating more than my fair share of sweets," Maureen explained as they wound their way toward Pearl Street. The street ran parallel to the beach, and one could glimpse the lake between the rambling old Victorian houses. Although the day had been hot and sunny, the air was now comfortable as the sun made its descent in the west, over the lake.

"Do you want to walk on the beach?" Esther asked. The heavy sand made a better workout. But she hoped not.

Maureen shook her head. "No. I don't want to deal with the sand right now. I've got to meet a client at ten tonight. She wants help redecorating her living room."

"Why so late?"

"She works twelve-hour shifts and doesn't get home until nine."

They walked a bit, and Maureen asked, "Are things better between you and Suzanne?"

"Somewhat. I'm hopeful things will continue to improve," Esther said, but the longer it went on, the less confident she felt. In their sisterly history, this had been the longest they'd gone over a disagreement.

"I can tell something's bothering you."

Esther could feel her brow wrinkling. "It's not that there's anything bothering me, it's that I've got something on my mind."

"And you want to divest yourself of it."

She nodded, relieved. Sometimes, Maureen just "got" her. "It has to do with Derrick."

"Oh no."

Esther was quick to explain. "It's nothing bad. He's done nothing wrong."

"I'm relieved to hear that."

Maureen picked up her pace and Esther had to walk faster to keep up. It made her wonder how many desserts Maureen had been eating.

Esther launched into her tale. "We've had a great time catching up. He's a nice guy. He even apologized for dumping me all those years ago."

"I hear a 'but' in there."

Esther stopped walking, which forced her cousin to stop as well. She had to catch her breath. "We've been doing different things, just seeing how it goes."

"And how does it go?"

Esther groaned. "We have absolutely nothing in common."

Maureen smiled sympathetically.

"He likes the beach, I hate it," Esther went on. "He likes karaoke, and I'd rather have my kidney removed in a back alley"—here Maureen burst out laughing—"I love bowling. Him, not so much."

"That's a definite dealbreaker," Maureen said seriously.

"I know, right? And I guess he and his son are big gamers. Xbox, I don't know. He asked me to join them." She stopped and asked her cousin, "Do I look like a gamer to you?"

Maureen laughed. "I can hear the disappointment in your voice."

"I've spent the last twenty-plus years romanticizing the past, only to find out that we're incompatible."

"It's not that you're incompatible," Maureen started, but when Esther stared at her with a lift to her eyebrows, she added, "Okay, his not liking bowling makes it a non-starter."

"Exactly."

"Can we start walking again?"

"Sure, I only stopped to catch my breath," Esther said.

As they walked, Maureen picked up the thread of their conversation. "It's been over two decades. You both grew up, and your interests developed and evolved."

"I wonder what would have happened if we had married. Would we have grown apart?"

"Marriage is tricky like that. You have to allow space for each other to have your own interests and hobbies and sometimes, one is growing and the other is not, or you're both growing and evolving but in different directions."

When Esther didn't say anything, Maureen asked, "Is this what you're worried about? That it wouldn't have worked out had you gotten married?"

"No, it isn't that. I feel like I wasted all this time, all these years thinking about what could have been, what should have been. Playing the what-if game."

"We all play the what-if game," Maureen said.

"Even you?"

"Sure. When I'm mad at Allan, I ask myself what if I'd married Elliot Jurgens instead."

"No way!" Esther laughed. "He owns the Cadillac dealership out on the highway."

Maureen wiggled her eyebrows. "I know. I had a terrible crush on him in high school."

Esther couldn't stop laughing. "I didn't know this."

"I never told anyone."

"You'd be driving a brand-new Cadillac every year," Esther teased.

"The sacrifices we make," Maureen said with a mock grimace. "Luckily for Allan, I'm not mad at him that much."

They walked on for a while, Esther mulling things over.

"Getting back to Derrick," Maureen said, "can I ask, were you expecting to resume a relationship with him?"

Esther sighed. "I don't know what I was expecting. The practicalities of that are impossible. He lives in Florida and has a son he's close to, and I'm up here. But now I guess it's not an issue, because we're not meant for each other."

"And you know what? That's okay. Maybe you can finally put this to rest," Maureen said.

"Maybe I can." For years, Esther had clung to the notion that she and Derrick had been soulmates. Back when they were young, she'd been so sure and confident that she and Derrick were not only a great fit but destined to be together. When he left, it became apparent that he didn't feel the same way, and it had shattered her.

"I have another question to ask."

"You're full of questions today," Esther joked.

"I am." Maureen giggled. "Looking back, I wonder if you took the breakup with Derrick harder because it wasn't long after your father's death."

It surprised Esther that her eyes stung. Even after all this time. She blinked several times in rapid succession. The feeling blindsided her. It was true. Her father's death and the breakup with Derrick had happened in a time span of eighteen months. Maybe she would have handled being dumped better if she hadn't been grieving her father. Those had been tumultuous times.

They reached the end of Pearl and took a shortcut over to Main, walking in the direction that would eventually bring them back to Maureen's house on Bluebell Lane.

"Having an Oprah moment here," Maureen said. "Maybe it was a good thing you ran into him and spent some time together."

"To see that I wasn't missing anything?"

Maureen pressed her lips together. "Not necessarily that. More like it's given you clarity."

Esther nodded. "I can do clarity."

Chapter Thirty-Seven

Esther tapped her fountain pen against her chin as she contemplated the apology in front of her. This one was a tough one. The client, named Jane, had let her best friend down in a big way. While her friend's husband was dying of cancer, she'd ghosted her because she didn't know what to do or say. Esther thought about this one for a while and decided to go for heartfelt. She hoped Jane could patch it up with her best friend. Esther always tried to think of how the wronged party might feel and took it from there. She thought honesty here was the best option.

Dear Karen,
I am so sorry. I'm sorry for not being there for you while Travis was dying. I'm sorry for letting you both down. I'm sorry for not being strong enough to stand by your side with my arm around you as you went through this most

difficult time in your life and marriage. I'm sorry I hurt you. I'm sorry I didn't stay true to our lifelong friendship. I hope someday you can forgive me.
  With love,
  Jane

She put the apology aside to revisit later. Her own sister was at the front of her mind. She tried to view things through Suzanne's eyes. Was Esther an expert on Suzanne and Ray and what made their marriage tick? Did she have a right to voice her opinion on Ray's behavior and call him out on it? Had Ray gotten a bad rap within the family because of her and her mother's opinion? And had all of this put Suzanne in the unenviable position of being torn between her husband and her mother and sister? *Argh*. She hated having to admit she was wrong. But answering the above questions honestly, she realized that she owed her sister an apology.

Esther dragged her feet on this for a good part of the day, mulling over how she would word her own apology. A professional apology maker, and here she was struggling with writing one for herself. She pulled out the notebook she used for her clients' apologies and started jotting down notes and ideas.

As uncomfortable as it made her feel, telling Suzanne she was sorry was the right thing to do. And sometimes doing the right thing caused discomfort. She wondered about that for a moment. Was that like a growing pain? Did that mean growth was happening? She sure hoped so.

Over a cup of coffee, she gathered her thoughts, reminding herself not to excuse her behavior but to offer a sincere apology. But she kept writing and then crossing out her lines until eventually she ripped out the page from her spiral notebook, balled it up, and tossed it on the floor, destined for the garbage. She sighed. This was hard. She didn't know how to word it. Finally, she pushed the notebook away, deciding a quick walk might clear her head.

The dog and the cats were curled up on the sofa and did not even lift their heads when she walked by. She locked the door behind her and headed into town. She hoped that by stretching her legs she could clear her head and better organize her thoughts.

The Quirk and the Quill came into sight, and she thought she'd buy a nice notecard to send to her sister. Any excuse to go into that shop. She pushed through the front door, savoring the scent of stationery, pens, pencils, and paper. It was her high.

"Hello, Esther. Here for your monthly birthday cards?" Loretta asked.

She hadn't been thinking about that, but while she was here, she might as well. There were only two birthdays in the family this month: Aunt Louise's and DeeDee's.

"You know me so well," Esther said with a laugh. With a wave, she headed down to the card aisle, where she spotted Debbie Melvin in the section for birthday cards for mothers. Debbie stood there, staring at the cards and biting her lip, her posture slumped.

"Hey, Deb, how are you?"

Debbie turned in her direction, and a smile appeared on her face. "Hi, Esther. How are things?"

"Good," Esther said. With a nod toward the cards, she said, "Is it your mother's birthday?"

"Tomorrow," Debbie said with a sigh. "Nothing like leaving things to the last minute."

To make her feel better, Esther said, "Some people work best under pressure."

Debbie snorted. She pulled out two cards and held them up. "This one's too flowery, and this one doesn't say enough."

"What about a funny card? I like them myself. Suzanne's kids try to outdo each other and see who can give me the funniest card for my birthday," Esther told her.

"My mother isn't exactly noted for her sense of humor."

Esther agreed with her but said nothing. For her entire life, Debbie had been in a no-win situation with her home life. It was amazing she turned out as normal as she did, quirks notwithstanding. She wondered if Debbie's siblings went through the same thing. Or did they have different kinds of wounds? If it were her, she would have left Lavender Bay a long time ago and not looked back.

"What brings you in here?" Debbie asked. The expression on her face suggested she needed to be thrown a lifeline. Or a distraction.

"I need a couple of cards as well." Unable to stand by idly, Esther said, "Can I help you pick out a card?"

"That would be great as I'm paralyzed with indecision. You know how she is."

Esther nodded. "I do."

"No matter what I choose . . ." Debbie's voice trailed off.

Mrs. Melvin should consider herself lucky to be getting a birthday card at all, all things considered, but Esther kept that to herself and opted for reassurance. "Look, all you can do is give her a card. How she responds to it, whatever she thinks about it, is on her. You have no control over her reaction."

Debbie's laugh was bitter. "Tell me about it."

"Once you hand her the birthday card, it's out of your hands. So stop worrying."

"I know you're right," Debbie said. "You should have been a counselor, Esther!"

Esther picked up three cards, read through them carefully, put them back, and chose another three. Debbie watched her, nibbling at her fingernail.

"Here you go," Esther said. "This one is perfect. Not too flowery and nothing about how wonderful she is. More of the sentiment of the giver, hoping she has a terrific day."

Debbie read it once, then a second time, and looked with uncertainty at the rest of the cards on display.

"It's good, Debbie, it's the best you can do," Esther told her. "Do you have to buy her a gift?"

"That's the easy part," Debbie said, her face relaxing. "She only wants lottery tickets and scratch-offs."

"That is easy," Esther agreed, surprised.

"Unless she doesn't win anything," Debbie said. "Then she complains about the duds."

There was no pleasing Mrs. Melvin.

Debbie looked again at the card rack. But Esther intervened.

"Nope, go check out. You've got a card. Your work here is done."

Debbie laughed and nodded. "You're right, Esther. Thanks for your help."

"Any time."

"I might go over to the Ink Stain and get a tattoo," Debbie said out of the blue.

Esther smiled, knowing Jim Sloane would be delighted to see her. "That's a good idea. You've been talking about it for some time, haven't you?"

She nodded. "I have." With a lift of the birthday card, she said, "Thanks again, Esther."

"Take care of yourself, Deb."

Debbie headed up to the checkout, and Esther turned her attention to her mission: She selected two birthday cards and found a lovely blank notecard with a field of sunflowers on the front of it for Suzanne. Perfect!

As she walked home, carrying the small paper bag of cards in her hand, she thought about Deb and the anxiety she had over selecting a birthday card for her mother. Why did family members treat each other so poorly? Why do that to a person you were supposed to love? The basic principle of the Hippocratic oath—do no harm—should be applied to families. With that in mind, she examined her own conscience and realized she hadn't always been a stellar example of that with regard to Suzanne. By the time she got home, she knew what she had to write.

Dear Suzanne,
Please accept this as a long overdue apology.
As much as I hate to admit it, my opinion and treatment of Ray has been both wrong and unfair all these years. I never thought about my behavior from your point

of view. Or his. It's one thing to not like someone, but it's another thing altogether to hurt the people you love. Long story short, I'm appalled at my own behavior.

I ask for your forgiveness. I miss my sister. I miss my best friend.

Love,
Esther

When she was finished, she walked Pebbles over to the post office and dropped the card into the collection box outside.

Two days later, she received a text from Suzanne: *Got your beautiful card. I know how difficult it must have been for you to write. All's well.* The text ended with a heart emoji.

Esther breathed out a huge sigh of relief.

Chapter Thirty-Eight

Esther sat outside in a pair of shorts and a T-shirt. The pool still had the solar cover over it, but she didn't feel like swimming. She was enjoying the moment: the peacefulness, the birds chirping, and the sound of the pool filter. The summer had been excellent, weatherwise. She couldn't ask for more. She was expecting Derrick. He was heading back to Florida the next day. It was time.

She heard the door behind her slide open and close, and Derrick appeared, smiling and tanned. He sported his summer uniform of a T-shirt, shorts, and deck shoes. He held his car keys in his hand.

She looked up, squinting and shielding her eyes from the sun, and smiled. "Hey there."

"Hey there yourself." He sat down in the chair next to her.

They'd seen each other the day before, taking a drive to Cheever, where they'd had lunch at a small bistro.

On the way out, Derrick had spotted a model train museum and with all the enthusiasm of a six-year-old on Christmas morning, asked Esther to go. Although not her thing and knowing it was two hours she wouldn't get back, she couldn't say no. In the end, he'd been happy with it, saying he wished his son were there with him.

"It's really quiet around here this morning, isn't it?" he said.

"I love it when it's like this. Would you like some coffee?"

He shook his head. "No thanks, I've already had two cups this morning."

They were interrupted by the sliding glass door opening and Becky poking her head out. "Esther, I'm going over to Sophie and Margret's now."

"Okay. What's the plan?"

Becky laughed. "The same as yesterday and the day before: we're going to the beach."

"Have fun. Hey, do you need any money?"

"Nope. I still have the money you gave me yesterday."

"Do you need me to pick you up later?"

Becky shook her head. "Suzanne said she'll drop me off after dinner."

"All right then, have fun."

"Bye, Esther. See you later."

The sliding door closed, and they were alone again.

"When is Becky going home?" Derrick asked.

"I'm flying down with her next week. School starts in the middle of August," Esther said, although she was sure Derrick already knew that, having raised his son in Florida.

"How's it going, having a houseguest?" he asked.

"Fine. She's a breeze. She's here in the morning, then she spends the day with Sophie and Margret, usually down at the beach. She goes to Suzanne's for dinner and then is here at night. Then we enjoy the universal hobby of watching movies and eating snacks together." Esther had spoken to Rose regularly, reassuring her that Becky was doing fine and having a great time.

"She going to be okay?" Derrick asked, having been filled in on the bullying.

Esther shrugged. "I hope so. That poor kid."

"There's nothing worse. High school is supposed to be the best time of your life, but maybe not for everyone."

"She's been talking about moving up here after graduation to go to college." Esther only hoped the girl could hold her own through the next few years. She'd already mentioned to Rose that Becky could transfer to the high school here, but Rose had said no and Esther understood her reasons perfectly.

"She plans ahead," Derrick said.

Esther smiled. Maybe it was an option or an exit for the girl. Maybe she needed to cling to that thought to get her through.

"Anyway, if that's what she wants, we'll make sure she gets it," Esther said. "She can live here with me. I've already told her that."

Derrick smiled. "As my mother used to say, you're a good egg, Esther."

She laughed, wondering how it came about to be describing people as eggs, good or otherwise. They made a few more minutes of small talk before she decided to approach the subject of his leaving in the morning. A cardinal flew by, his red feathers vibrant. Esther made a mental note to look into getting a bird feeder.

"Are you all ready for tomorrow?" she asked.

"I am."

"Do you have a ride to the airport?"

"Actually, when I drop off the rental, I'll grab the shuttle to the airport.

"Good." She would have offered but was secretly glad she didn't have to, if only to be spared any awkwardness. "I imagine you're anxious to get home and see your son."

"I am," he said. "Although I'm on the Xbox with him every day, it's not the same."

"Of course not."

"I feel bad leaving you, Esther," he said.

"Why?"

"I don't know. I don't want you to feel like I'm dumping you again."

That was sweet of him. "I promise you, I don't think that at all."

"I'm glad to hear that. We've had some fun."

"We have," she agreed. "It's been great to catch up."

"And it's been fun hanging out."

"It has."

"Can I ask your honest opinion about things? About us?"

She laughed. "Give me a minute. I didn't know there was going to be a quiz."

Derrick burst out laughing. "That's one of the things I really like about you, Esther. Your sense of humor."

"And I like that you always laugh at my jokes."

"Seriously, we get along so well, just like the old days," Derrick said.

Eventually, she said, "We do."

"I sense hesitation there."

She proceeded carefully. Her tendency to be blunt and honest could be misconstrued. And she certainly didn't want to hurt him unnecessarily. "When we broke up, I took it really hard."

"I did apologize for that," he pointed out.

She nodded. "You did. And I appreciate that." She looked off into the distance, trying to figure out how to say what she wanted to say. "And I'm grateful for running into you because it's given me some perspective."

"Uh-oh. That sounds bad."

She laughed. "Not at all. In the twenty-five years since we've seen each other, our lives have gone in different directions. You've been busy raising a son. And I've been up here, well, bowling," she said in an attempt to inject some humor into the situation. It worked, because he chuckled.

"Anyway," she continued, "we've evolved to the point where I no longer recognize the girl I used to be back then. You and I have different interests now." She refrained from saying they had nothing in common. There was no need for overkill.

"It's true. I'm not a big fan of bowling."

Esther grinned. "And that's all right. I can admit now to hating karaoke."

Now he was bent over laughing. When he stopped, he said, "Once I leave, you'll never have to pick up a microphone again."

She lifted her hands heavenward and exclaimed, "Hallelujah!"

They settled in contented amusement for a few moments before Derrick spoke up. "You know, I thought you might suggest you'd want a long-distance relationship."

Esther grinned. "Nice to see your ego is intact," she teased.

"So we'll always be friends?"

"Of course." But she couldn't see keeping in touch. Their relationship had now come to a definitive conclusion. There was no reason for him to come back to Lavender Bay now that his parents were gone. And she couldn't see seeking him out in Florida when she was there on vacation. And that was okay.

He stood to leave. "I better get going. I've got a few errands to run before I leave tomorrow."

Esther walked with him around to the front. They stood next to his truck and somehow ended up in a hug.

"Well, goodbye, Esther."

"Goodbye, Derrick."

She waved him off as he pulled away. She waited in her driveway until his truck disappeared down the street.

She turned to walk into the house, thinking she might like to go for a swim after all.

It was time to move on with her life.

Chapter Thirty-Nine

Two nights later, Esther sat alone in her backyard as twilight settled in around her. The noise of the crickets drowned out the pool filter. A citronella candle burned on the table, but its efficacy was doubtful as every once in a while, she had to swat away a mosquito. Pebbles sat at her feet, looking around.

Her cousin Nadine had taken Becky, Sophie, and Margret to a drive-in over in Cheever. The three girls had mentioned at the last coffee morning that they'd never been to a drive-in, and Nadine had made it her mission that they should experience it.

Esther was in for the night and had made a pitcher of margaritas for herself. Lou had been on her mind lately, and she had been thinking about giving him a call. There was still unfinished business there.

"Esther?"

Suzanne.

She held up her drink. "Grab yourself a glass, sis," Esther said without turning around. She topped up her glass as her sister sat down and set a margarita glass on the table. As Esther filled her sister's glass to the top, she asked, "You didn't want salt around the rim?"

"Nah." Suzanne took a sip, and her eyes widened. "Wow, this is strong."

"Be glad, then, that you live within walking distance."

"Mom called me," Suzanne said. "She told me Derrick went back to Florida."

"That's right. He left yesterday."

"How do you feel about that?"

Esther shrugged. "Fine, actually. It turns out after all this time, we have nothing in common."

Suzanne made no comment.

Pebbles stood up and walked around the other side of the pool to inspect something.

Esther stood up. "Hold that thought, I've got taco dip inside. Be right back."

"Do you need some help?" Suzanne asked.

"Nope."

Pebbles ran around from the other side of the pool and followed Esther into the house.

Balancing the tray of dip and the bag of chips in one hand, Esther pulled open the sliding glass door. Pebbles bolted between her legs to get outside, causing Esther to teeter on her feet.

"Pebbles!"

But the dog had already landed at Esther's chair, vigilant, knowing snacks were going to be consumed and hoping someone would throw her the odd chip.

Suzanne laughed. "She's like a kid."

"Yeah, she is."

Esther set the taco dip and the bag of chips down on the table between the two chairs. Once they were settled, they reached for the bag of chips and began scooping up dip. Neither said anything at first, as if they needed the fortification of comfort food for what was sure to be a painful but hopefully heartfelt conversation. Although Esther dreaded this, she knew it was important to clear the air. Their mother was right; it had gone on long enough.

Suzanne ate a few chips with dip, brushed off her hands, and sipped her drink. "I'll start the ball rolling," she said.

Esther thought it was a good analogy, given her love of bowling.

"I'll take a page from your book, and I'll be blunt," Suzanne started. "You don't like my husband."

Esther went to protest but Suzanne cut her off.

"Esther, if we're going to do this, we need to be honest with each other," Suzanne said.

Esther nodded. "You're right," she admitted. "Ray wouldn't be one of my top people."

There, she'd said it. It was out there.

"Can you give me a specific reason?" Suzanne asked, munching on a chip.

Esther scooped up more dip, shoving it into her mouth. She arranged the thoughts swirling around in her head. "I don't like the way he treats you, plain and simple. I think you deserve better."

"In what ways don't you like the way he treats me?"

"You know. He's controlling, Suzanne, you must realize that."

Her sister nodded slowly. "I do."

"But you put up with it." Esther kept her voice neutral, trying not to display any of the frustration she'd harbored for years over this.

Suzanne was silent for a few moments, thoughtful. Finally, she said, "I know he's controlling. It's an issue, I won't lie."

"Then why do you put up with it?" Exasperation crept into Esther's voice.

"Because I understand why he is the way he is."

"You do? Why?" It came as a surprise to Esther that there might be a reason for Ray's behavior.

"You know that Ray's mother walked out on the family when Ray was nine," Suzanne said.

Esther nodded. For whatever reason, Ray's mother had had enough, or maybe she wasn't cut out for marriage and motherhood. In any case, she walked out one day while her kids were at school and was never seen again.

"That incident—for lack of a better word—has affected Ray's whole life."

Esther wasn't wholly convinced. "We lost Dad when we were pretty young, and we didn't turn into control freaks."

Suzanne tilted her head and looked at her sister. "Maybe we didn't become control freaks, but maybe Dad's premature death resulted in other things."

"What do you mean?"

"Do you ever wonder why you love bowling so much?"

"I don't know. I love it, that's all."

"Esther, you're obsessed with bowling. But Dad loved it too, and maybe it's a way for you to stay connected to him."

"I suppose. I just assumed I'd inherited the bowling gene." She took a sip of her margarita. "I get that it must have been awful for Ray to lose his mother, but why is that any worse than us losing our father?"

Suzanne shook her head. "It wasn't the same. And I don't think you can compare the two. Dad didn't choose to leave us. He died. It was unexpected. I'm sure if Dad had a choice, he would have preferred to stay."

Esther didn't say anything, already intuiting where her sister was going with this.

"Ray's mother chose to leave them. He was nine. Old enough to remember and be wounded by it and young enough to blame himself and not fully understand."

"That doesn't excuse Ray's present behavior," Esther countered.

"I'm not excusing his behavior, I'm explaining it," Suzanne said. "Abandonment by the mother has to be one of the most difficult things for children to recover from. That's my theory, but what do I know? Think about it. The one person who's supposed to love you unconditionally, and at the very least stick around, chooses to leave. It has messed up Ray's whole family in some way. Kudos to his father for trying to hold it all together, because that's all he could do."

Esther conceded those points.

"And now, Ray has been acting like this for so long, it's become an ingrained habit. Half the time, I don't think he even realizes what he's doing."

By now, Esther felt emboldened to speak her mind. "But how do you stand it? Him controlling your every move?"

"Does it get on my nerves? Yes. Does it cause problems? Yes. I feel like I'm torn between my husband and you and Mom. Deep down, I think Ray worries every time I walk out the door that I'm not coming back. Logically, that's ridiculous. But since when do affairs of the heart ever have anything to do with logic?"

"How can you live like that?"

Suzanne sighed. "I've done it for so long I don't know anything else. Is it right? No. But I understand why he's doing it."

"And this business where you have to wait on him hand and foot. I mean really, Suzanne, it's a bit much. Him ordering you around all the time to get him something."

"That doesn't bother me too much."

"Because you're used to it? It's hard to watch him issuing orders to you all the time."

Suzanne remained quiet.

"And what about the kids?" Esther continued. "The girls will think this is how it is, that men are controlling and women exist to be at their beck and call. And the boys will grow up to repeat what they learn at home. This is how they'll treat women."

Suzanne flinched. "I've thought about that."

"And?"

She swirled her drink around in her glass, staring at it as if the whirlpool of the beverage held all the answers. "I don't like it."

This is where Esther became exasperated. "Suzanne, I don't understand you. You're concerned about Ray's behavior and the effect it has on the kids, but you do nothing about it."

"I know," Suzanne said. "Sometimes I don't know what to do."

"Not making a decision is a decision in and of itself," Esther pointed out.

"I know, I know," Suzanne said. She pursed her lips and looked out over the pool.

"Let me ask you this. Do you love Ray?"

"Of course I love him," Suzanne responded, surprised at the question.

"Oh."

Suzanne laughed. "Why does that surprise you?"

Esther shrugged and admitted, "I don't know."

"You think that because you don't like my husband, I must not like him either. And if I don't like him, then there's no way I can be in love with him. Right?"

When she put it like that, it sounded convoluted.

"I'm not crazy in love with Ray the way I was when we were first married," Suzanne said.

Esther frowned.

"Trust me, that kind of passion and intensity is hard to sustain after a long time," Suzanne said knowingly. "But we've had four children together, and therefore we have a very important shared history. I'm not saying it's easy, because it isn't. Ray and I have different ideas of how a marriage should work, and that has caused a lot of friction."

"What do you want to happen?" Esther asked.

Her sister didn't answer her question right away. When she finally spoke, she said, "I know you want me to get divorced—"

Esther cut her off. "That's not true. What I want is for you to be happy and well-treated. But it doesn't matter what I want, it's what you want."

"He's not a bad guy. Yes, he's controlling, but he has good points too," Suzanne said. "He'd do anything I asked of him. He's a good father. He adores the kids, and they adore him."

Begrudgingly, Esther had to admit that Ray did do things with his kids, spent time with them. Was involved and interested in their lives.

"He doesn't try to control the kids?" Esther pressed.

"Not like he tries to control me. And if he were to try that, the girls are old enough that they'd call him out on it."

"Good for them."

They went quiet for a moment before Esther picked up the thread of the conversation again. "He doesn't want you to work. You've got that college degree and you've never used it." Her sister was well-educated and intelligent, with a lot to offer.

"Actually, I love being a stay-at-home mom," Suzanne admitted.

"And there's nothing wrong with that if that's your choice. But if you were forced into it . . ."

Suzanne started laughing. "To set the record straight, Ray did not force me to stay at home or have kids."

"All right." Esther thought for a moment. "What do you want, Suzanne? And let your answer reflect your wants and needs, not the needs of your husband and your kids."

"Hmm," Suzanne said. "I'd like Ray to be less controlling and trust me more. Once the boys are older, I might like to go back to work, even if it's only part time."

Esther nodded. "That's a start." She stood to refresh their drinks. Suzanne took the bag of chips and folded it in half to close it.

"Now, the question is, what are you going to do about it?" Esther asked.

Suzanne shrugged. "I don't know."

"Suzanne, you can't be wishy-washy about this." Esther narrowed her eyes at her sister. "He doesn't hit you, does he?"

"Of course not!"

"Thank goodness for that. But just because he doesn't hit you, that doesn't mean there isn't abuse going on," Esther pointed out.

"I know." Suzanne finally said, "No matter what I decide, I need your support. I need to know that you have my back."

"You got it. But it's conditional. If you continue to allow yourself to be treated like a doormat, then I'm going to speak up. To Ray."

Suzanne nodded. "Understood." Their shared silence was broken by Suzanne. "Can you tell me why it bothers you now?"

Esther sighed. "I think the breakup with Lou triggered something. Apparently, it bothered me more than I thought it would. And when you kept cancelling our plans, I felt abandoned. I wanted to talk to you about it." She didn't add, *I needed to talk to you about it.*

Suzanne was shame-faced. "Esther, I am so sorry."

Esther waved her apology away. "Don't worry about it."

"I'm glad you told me this. It's important to know that my own actions affect other people. Again, I'm sorry I let you down."

Now that the air was cleared between them, Esther felt lighter. She hoped her sister felt the same way.

"Speaking of Lou? Any hope there?" Suzanne asked.

"What are you, like a cheerleader for Lou or something?" Esther asked.

"Maybe. I like him. But more importantly, I like him for you."

"One thing I did learn hanging out with Derrick is that Lou and I have a lot of common interests."

"That's code for 'He really likes bowling.' "

Esther couldn't help but laugh, almost choking on her drink. She cleared her throat, wiped her eyes, and said, "Something like that."

Chapter Forty

Later that evening, happy that she and her sister had patched things up and feeling brave, Esther called Lou and asked him to come over. While she waited, she sat at her kitchen table, working on the roster for the fall schedule of the bowling league. Her current team was made up of her cousins Nadine, whose game continued to improve; DeeDee, whose aptitude had been a pleasant surprise; and Maureen, who'd already informed her of two Saturdays she'd be missing because of going away with Allan for conferences. Esther's mother and her aunt were down as alternates. They usually showed up anyway for team night, if only to offer a running commentary, giggling amongst themselves like Wilma Flintstone and Betty Rubble.

Pebbles sat on the sofa, her chin resting on the back of it. She looked out the front window, vigilant, like she was a member of the neighborhood watch group.

Before Lou even knocked at the door, Esther knew he'd arrived. It started with Pebbles. She had this "Lou" signal. Her tail started wagging wildly, she jumped around, whining, and then she dashed to the door as if the house were on fire.

Esther pushed back her chair and headed to the door. Before she opened it, she took a deep breath. Her palms were clammy. But as soon as she opened the door and saw Lou standing there with his beautiful wavy gray hair, all her anxiety faded away.

"Come on in, Lou," she said, stepping back to allow him to enter.

"Hello, Es, it's good to see you," he said. He came in and reached forward to pet Pebbles. "Hey, Pebs, missed you too."

Deciding there were too many mosquitoes outside, they made themselves comfortable in the living room. Pebbles jumped up and settled down beside Lou.

"Would you like something to drink? Something to eat?" Esther asked.

"No, Es, I'm good."

Esther made herself comfortable at the opposite end of the sofa. "I called you over to ask for another chance."

He looked dumbfounded and said nothing at first. One of the cats, Sylvia, appeared and meowed at Lou, jumping up on the arm of the sofa and sitting next to him.

"Another chance?" he finally repeated.

Now she was nervous because she didn't know whether she'd been unclear or whether he was stalling for time.

"Yes," she said. "You and me. A reboot. Esther and Lou two-point-O,"

"Oh, you want to get back together," he said.

"I do," Esther confirmed, painfully aware that he still hadn't said he was interested.

"What about Derrick Radich?" Lou stroked Sylvia's back, and she closed her eyes and purred.

"Derrick and I spent some time together this summer, but it was nothing serious. We were only hanging out. Catching up before he went back to Florida."

"Is he coming back?" Lou asked without looking at her.

"No, I don't think so," Esther said. "And even if he did, it wouldn't matter. A lot of time has passed since I'd last seen him, and we've changed as people."

"Well, that's what time does to you. If he hadn't changed, would you have called me over?"

"Even if *he* hadn't changed, I have. There were times when I was with him and thinking of you."

When Lou didn't say anything, she said, "I miss you, Lou." That was the truth. She missed his sense of humor and their easy, effortless companionship.

"I miss you too, Es, very much. When you invited me over, I did some serious thinking about you and me." He looked at her and gave her that easy smile of his. "Maybe it was wrong of me to pressure you into something you didn't want to do. I shouldn't have pushed so hard for us to move in together."

She said nothing. That seemed like a long time ago. "It isn't right or wrong. It's that at that time, we wanted different things from the relationship. I mean, why should you settle?"

"I never settled being with you," he said. "But I'll say this, Es, you're the only one for me." He paused. "Shall we try again?"

She grinned. "Are you asking me out on a date?"

"A date. Seeing each other again."

She didn't have to think about it. "Yes, I'd like that."

They spent the next half hour catching up and making plans for the fall and winter. As it was getting late, Lou stood to leave.

On his way out, with his hand on the doorknob, he said, "Fun fact: the first bowling alley in the White House was installed by Harry Truman. He, Nixon, Bush, and Obama were all bowlers."

"I did not know that."

"And on that note, I'll leave you." He paused. "Will I call you tomorrow?"

She nodded. "Yes."

Chapter Forty-One

Aunt Louise's house was shrouded in darkness when they all arrived late Saturday night after going out to dinner at the Annacotty Room for her birthday. Instead of calling it a night, they'd decided to go back to her house for coffee.

They filed inside through the back door, which led to the kitchen. Louise turned on the lights, and her one-eyed rescue cat, Peter, hobbled over to her on his three legs, his eye barely open as if they'd disturbed him from a deep sleep.

Louise bent over and stroked him behind his ears. "Hello, my love, did we wake you?" After a few seconds, the cat, having been given a little treat and satisfied that all was well, settled into his bed near the kitchen heater.

Everyone did something. Louise tackled the coffeemaker, and Maureen prepared the stovetop percolator. Because of the time of night, decaf was the choice. No need for any of them to be awake all night because they were overcaffeinated. Nadine pulled out spoons and forks, and Angie set some baked goods on trays. Esther brought the sugar and creamer to the table, and Suzanne brought over a stack of dessert plates, while DeeDee made sure there were enough mugs for everyone.

Esther sat at one end of the table, and Suzanne took the seat next to her and smiled at her.

"Ray take the kids home?" Esther asked.

"Yep, it's a little late for Patrick and Jason. And Ray figured this would be a girls' thing."

It was a smaller group than their usual Sunday morning numbers, but Esther thought with only the eight of them, it was cozier and more intimate. Once they were all seated around the farmhouse table, Maureen said to her mother and her aunt, "Let me get a picture of the two of you."

Louise pulled her chair next to Gail, who sat at the head of the table. "I'm ready." She gave an exaggerated smile. Her sister looked at her, did a double take, and shook her head.

"Let me put on some lipstick," Gail said.

Louise laughed. "Forget that. It's eleven o'clock at night."

"What does the time have to do with it?" Gail asked. They looked at each other and burst out laughing as if there was some private joke going on between the two of them.

Louise gave Gail a gentle nudge. "Come on, smile for the camera."

After Maureen took several shots, Gail reached over, took her sister's face in her hands, and gave her a noisy smooch on the cheek. "Happy Birthday, Louise!"

Louise giggled. "Thanks, sis."

Maureen looked at the photos she'd just taken. "These are lovely. We'll have to get them printed and framed."

The plate of baked goods remained untouched. Finally, Esther caved and reached for one. "I hate to say this, but I'm actually hungry," she said.

"You'd think you hadn't eaten in a week," Suzanne teased.

Esther laughed. "I know, I know."

Maureen yawned. "It warms the cockles of my heart to see the two of you speaking to each other again."

Esther grinned. "Nice turn of phrase there, Maureen."

"I'm impressed myself," she said with a mock self-satisfied smile.

"Maureen's right," Angie said. "It's good to see the two of you back together."

"It was only a little glitch," Suzanne reassured them. She looked at her sister, who nodded.

"Whatever it was, I'm glad it's behind you," Louise said.

Gail looked heavenward. "It's an answer to a prayer."

Louise leaned into her and said with emphasis, "A lot of prayers."

Esther had already decided that no matter what happened, she would never let anything come between her and Suzanne again. She would never go so long without speaking to her sister. She only had to look to her mother and her aunt for the example.

"Mom, I have a question for you and Aunt Louise," Esther said.

They both looked at her.

"Did the two of you ever have a serious argument? Did you ever have a fight?" she asked.

Gail and Louise looked at each other and giggled.

"Of course we've fought and argued," said Gail.

"We are sisters, after all," Louise added with a yawn.

The two of them were met with blank stares around the table.

Esther was the first to speak. "I don't think I ever remember a harsh word between you . . ."

Maureen shook her head. "I don't either."

Gail shrugged and said with a sniff, "We don't do that stuff anymore."

"We were pretty nuclear as teenagers, though," Louise said.

Angie raised an eyebrow. "I can't imagine it."

"It's true. We fought a lot." Gail appeared thoughtful. "Sometimes it was like the OK Corral at our house." This brought on another round of laughing between them.

Esther smiled. "You can tell it's getting late. They're getting giddy."

"The two of you are like soulmates," Suzanne said.

DeeDee shook her head. "It's more than that. They're like twin flames."

Gail raised her eyebrows and said, "Oooh, I like that. Twin flames."

"Me too." Louise smiled.

"So what happened?" Nadine asked.

Louise looked at Gail. "Should we tell them?"

Gail's expression turned somber. "Probably. It was fifty years ago."

Louise nodded. "You're right, of course, but then you always are."

"Wait, something happened?" Suzanne asked.

"Like a catalyst?" Esther asked.

Gail smiled. "I like that word too." She looked at her sister, who yawned again. "We'll save it for another time. It's getting late and the birthday girl is tired."

Angie protested. "Aw, come on. You can't leave us hanging."

"That's why they call it a cliffhanger," Louise said with a knowing smile.

Gail stood. "It can wait until the next time. It's too long of a story to start now."

Her word was final; they'd have to wait. Quickly, everyone pitched in and cleared the table and loaded the dishwasher so Louise wouldn't have to deal with a mess in the morning.

"It's Sunday tomorrow, but we're not getting together for coffee morning, are we?" DeeDee asked.

"No, not necessary," Gail said. "I'm sleeping in tomorrow."

"Me too," her sister added.

The cousins all went their separate ways, each one more curious than the other to hear Gail and Louise's story.

Chapter Forty-Two

October

Esther reread the article in *The Lavender Bay Chronicles* several times, her excitement building with each read. She set the newspaper down, picked up her phone, and pressed Lou's phone number from her contact list.

"Esther! I've been expecting your call," he said.

Was her boyfriend now a mind reader? she thought wryly.

Lou continued. "I think I know why you're calling." She could almost see him smiling on the other end of the phone.

"You do?"

"You've seen the article in the newspaper about the couples' bowling league."

"I have," she admitted. It was just the thing she was looking for. It wasn't starting up until after Christmas. And the beautiful thing was, someone else was organizing it. All she had to do was show up with Lou and her bowling ball. No more strong-arming relatives and friends into bowling with her. She could barely contain her glee. "It's like a dream come true."

Lou chuckled. "Too bad it's over in Cheever."

"I don't mind the drive if you don't," she said.

"No, I don't mind, Esther."

"Would you be interested?"

"Of course. Sign us up," he said good-naturedly.

"See you after work?" she asked.

"I'll be there."

They hung up, and Esther did a few more things before she sat down to work. It was her turn to cook dinner tonight. She'd already seared some meat and put it in the crockpot with potatoes, carrots, and onions. She had a surprise for Lou. Since they'd gotten back together, Lou had been true to his word and had not once mentioned the idea of moving in together. Hadn't even hinted at it.

But she'd take it a step further. Forget about moving in. For the first time in Esther's life, she was ready to talk about marriage.

Because when you knew, you knew.

The following Saturday, Suzanne popped in between ferrying her kids to and from their activities. She was dressed in jeans and a fleece pullover, a reminder that the hot weather was behind them. Esther welcomed the visit. Suzanne looked out the back window at the pool. "You know summer is truly over when the pool is closed up," she said.

"That's for sure." It was always a little sad not to be able to sit outside around the pool in the summer sunshine. But the pool had its season, and right now Esther was in full swing with her bowling team. "Tea or coffee?" she asked.

Suzanne shook her head. "No thanks. I've already had three cups this morning. If I drink any more coffee, I'll be jittery."

Esther chuckled. "I get it."

They sat down on the sofa, displacing the cats and Pebbles. The dog didn't seem to mind. She sat on the floor in front of Suzanne, wagging her tail and staring at her. Suzanne couldn't resist leaning forward and showing her some affection.

"What's new?" Esther asked. She curled up with her legs beneath her at the other corner of the sofa.

"Funny you should ask," Suzanne said. She leaned back and clasped her hands in her lap. "Ray and I have had some conversations."

"And?"

"He's suggested we go to marriage counseling," Suzanne told her.

"It was his idea?" Esther couldn't hide her disbelief.

Her sister nodded. "It was. I told him how I felt about things and how I understood why he acts the way he does. At first, he disputed what I was saying until I was able to give him examples of his controlling behavior. Then he suggested we try counseling."

"That's a step in the right direction." Esther was hopeful for them both.

"I think so. I also very gently suggested that he see a therapist by himself to deal with the issues surrounding his mother's abandonment."

"That's also a good idea. How did he take that?"

"Initially, he was resistant. Said there was nothing wrong with him and he didn't need counseling for that. But then a couple of days ago, he admitted that he probably could use some help. He'd spoken to his sister, who apparently saw a therapist years ago and encouraged him to go."

"That's great," Esther said honestly. Since their last conversation, she'd given a lot of thought to Ray's abandonment by his mother, and she found her attitude toward Ray softening a bit. Maybe children weren't as resilient as everyone said they were.

Suzanne continued. "I told him it was important for me to be able to keep my plans with you and Mom. That he can't expect me to change my plans just because he's feeling needy and is afraid I won't return."

"Who is this person? I hardly know her," Esther teased.

"He wasn't happy about it." Suzanne pursed her lips.

"He'll get used to it," Esther said.

"I'm hoping the counseling will help."

Esther concluded that she only had a general idea what went on in a marriage, that she really had no clue as to the day-to-day happenings and therefore was unqualified to provide comment or opinion.

But all that was about to change.

Chapter Forty-Three

The Following Spring

It was a beautiful day. Although the air was cool, the sun was bright and warm. Esther pushed through the door of Coffee Girl and spotted Suzanne already seated at a table. She approached and said, "Sorry I'm late. Pebbles decided that today was going to be the day she'd actually go after a squirrel."

Suzanne laughed. "Oh no. Did she catch him?"

Esther scoffed. "Of course not. I think it was all for show, trying to impress me."

Things had been going well. Suzanne and Ray were still going to counseling and experiencing growing pains in their marriage, which they were soldiering through. And Suzanne had only canceled one meet-up since last fall, when she and her kids all came down with a stomach bug.

Esther looked around and asked, "Did you order?"

Suzanne nodded. "I did. I ordered your usual as well."

"That's great, thanks," Esther said, and she pulled out the chair across from her sister and sat.

"It won't be long now," Suzanne said.

"Nope. I'm starting to get nervous. I'm a little long in the tooth to be a June bride."

"Nonsense! You're never too old to be a bride!" Suzanne was adamant in her opinion.

Esther had asked Lou to marry her. His complete surprise had delighted Esther almost as much as his immediate "yes." It was going to be a small wedding, just his family and hers. She liked to think of it like another coffee morning but with the exchange of vows. When she'd told Rose, her cousin was excited to have a reason to come back to Lavender Bay sooner rather than later. Esther had then texted Becky to let her know that nothing had changed regarding their plan for her to return for the summer, that there would be plenty of room for her to stay no matter what. Esther and Lou had yet to decide where they were going to live. It made sense to Esther for him to move into her house as she had the pool. But there was also a part of her that wanted a new home for the two of them: a place they could start their lives together.

"You have no idea how happy it makes me to see you wearing Grammy's ring," Suzanne said.

Esther held up her hand. Being the oldest granddaughter, their grandmother's ring, a trio of three diamonds, not too big and not too small, had been given to her. When Esther and Lou had announced their engagement—at a coffee morning at Aunt Louise's house—Gail immediately went home and retrieved the ring. The gold band was currently at the jeweler's getting polished up and resized.

"It's wonderful," Suzanne gushed. "You know how much we all love Lou."

"I do," Esther said, smiling. "So tell me, what's new?"

Suzanne launched into a diatribe about her family and Esther listened, always interested in what was going on in her nieces' and nephews' lives.

The two sisters went silent as Edna Knickerbocker and Edith Bermingham took the table next to them and sat down together.

"Well, that's nothing short of miraculous," Suzanne whispered.

"Hello, girls," Edna said with a wave.

"Hi, Mrs. Knickerbocker, Mrs. B," they replied.

Joel, their server, brought Esther and Suzanne's order over. As he removed their coffees and plates from his tray, Esther caught part of the conversation between Mrs. Knickerbocker and Mrs. B.

"This is a lovely time of year, isn't it? With all the flowers and leaves coming out," Edith observed.

"It is," Edna agreed.

"I've got a silver birch that's my favorite tree in the yard," Edith told her.

"I do too! Remember what Dad used to say about the silver birch?"

Edith picked up the thread. "Yes, I do. The leaves are first off in the fall and last on in the spring."

"Let me know if you need anything else," Joel said to Suzanne and Esther before leaving their table. Esther sipped her coffee and thought about the two elderly women next to them. If Edna and Edith could start talking to one another after sixty years, then she and Suzanne should have no problem at all with whatever life handed them in the future.

She continued to get snippets of their conversation, talking about things they both seemed to have an interest in. Maybe that's how friendship started. With simple common ground.

SIGN UP FOR MY NEWSLETTER

To stay up to date with new releases and receive exclusive bonus material, sign up for my newsletter at www.michelebrouder.com

Also By Michele Brouder

The Lavender Bay Chronicles
The Inn at Lavender Bay
Lost and Found in Lavender Bay
Second Chances in Lavender Bay
New Beginnings in Lavender Bay
Looking Back in Lavender Bay
Sisters and Friends in Lavender Bay (Coming in October 2025)

Hideaway Bay
Coming Home to Hideaway Bay
Meet Me at Sunrise
Moonlight and Promises
When We Were Young
One Last Thing Before I Go
The Chocolatier of Hideaway Bay
Now and Forever

Escape to Ireland
A Match Made in Ireland

Her Fake Irish Husband
Her Irish Inheritance
A Match for the Matchmaker
Home, Sweet Irish Home
An Irish Christmas
The Happy Holidays
A Whyte Christmas
This Christmas
A Wish for Christmas
One Kiss for Christmas
A Wedding for Christmas
Audiobooks
Coming Home to Hideaway Bay
Meet Me at Sunrise
All books available in ebook, paperback, and large print paperback. Audiobooks coming soon.

www.ingramcontent.com/pod-product-compliance
Lightning Source LLC
Chambersburg PA
CBHW020350080526
44584CB00014B/970